Penguin Special S221

What's Wrong with British Industry?

D1337834

Rex Malik

What's Wrong with British Industry?

Penguin Books

Penguin Books Ltd, Harmondsworth,
Middlesex

Penguin Books Inc., 3300 Clipper Mill Road,
Baltimore 11, Md, U.S.A.

Penguin Books Pty Ltd, Ringwood,
Victoria, Australia

Published in Penguin Books 1964

Copyright © Rex Malik, 1964

Made and printed in Great Britain by
Cox and Wyman Ltd, London, Reading,
and Fakenham

Set in Monotype Times

This book is sold subject to the condition
that it shall not, by way of trade, be lent,
re-sold, hired out, or otherwise
disposed of without the publisher's consent
in any form of binding or cover other
than that in which it is published

Contents

'Those who can't stand the heat of the fire, should get the hell out of the kitchen.'

Attributed to President Truman

'We can only grow at the proper speed we should grow if we make full use of all our resources and, above all, of our human resources of skill and brain power. There is no room in rapidly expanding Britain for any artificial limitations on the growth of production, or upon the expansion and training of skill. There is no room in an expanding Britain for restrictive practices of capital or labour. There is no room for unnecessary limitation on the training of our young people. There is no room for the man who is frightened to change, who wants to stay doing the same thing for the rest of his life. There is no room for the man who thinks research and development and new ideas are something all very well for the long-haired boys but not good enough for him. Above all there is no room in a really vigorously expanding economy for people who are not prepared to face competition and to face it squarely and honestly.'

R. Maudling to the Conservative Party Conference, 1962

Acknowledgements

It is more than difficult to acknowledge all the people who have helped to make this book possible, for I cannot remember them all. There are those whose companies appear in it: without them I should have had little material to use. There are the papers and journals to which I have contributed who made some of my studies possible. Among them I should like to single out the now extinct *Scope*, *The Times Review of Industry & Technology*, and Westminster Press Provincial Newspapers. There are, too, many people who have provided me with often invaluable information, unfortunately too many to mention by name, though they may recognize some of the points they made.

And then there are those who have spared me considerable time to discuss some of these specific problems, and those who have read all or parts of my manuscript: Mr Richard Bing, Brigadier J. Clemow, Dr F. E. Jones, Mr Clive Jenkins, Mr Andrew Robertson, Mr Nicholas A. H. Stacey, Mr Donald G. Stokes, and Mr Avison Wormald. It should be unnecessary to write that this does not mean to say they approve of all I have written, or even that they agree with any part of it. Their suggestions, arguments, and criticisms, however, have proved invaluable.

Lastly, I wish to acknowledge my debt to my wife who typed the many versions of the manuscript, and is the only person in our family who can ever remember where the apostrophes go.

Introduction

First, what this book is not. It is not a fair, exhaustive, heavily documented, and unreadable treatise. Nor have I taken the line that there are few of us who can understand what is going on, and that the general public needs protection from uncomfortable truths unless they are well wrapped up in clichés. Nor yet have I attempted to 'reveal all', for the simple reason that I lay no claim to know it all. I know enough about industry to be well aware of this book's shortcomings: I have not seriously discussed labour relations or trade unions (for which see Eric Wigham's authoritative Penguin Special, *What's Wrong with the Unions?*), the nationalized industries, the relations between manufacturing industry and the City, our transport problems, the inhibiting effect of our crazy tax system – or many other topics which could easily fit into its framework and themselves deserve further study.

I have however followed my own interests and mined, however ineffectively, some of the fields of activity which I have been covering both here and in Continental Europe during the last few years. Indeed, this work has part of its origins in a series of articles written in 1961 for *The Times Review of Industry* on the European Chemical Industry (reprinted as a pamphlet in 1962). What struck me then was the difference in atmosphere between the Continent and the United Kingdom, and nowhere was this more evident than in managerial circles. Put crudely, the difference was simply that they were awake, while we were not.

It is nowadays the fashion to impugn motives and intentions to our élite (a shorthand term, since we do not of course, have an élite in the real sense of the term. This is something which I hope become apparent). The case I am arguing, however, is not concerned with honesty, either financial or otherwise. It deals with ability.

What I have set out to do then is to be unfair to practically everybody. Though this is largely a polemic it has a basis of fact, and the first should not be allowed to detract from the second: this is what British industry looks like to one person who has observed not just British firms but also many of their foreign counterparts. Some of the topics in these pages have been ventilated during the last few months, but I hope people will persevere with me if I discuss them once again, even if I should have come to them in my own way. But no one should imagine that ventilation is any substitute for action. All it does is keep these problems before the public eye – and, one hopes, hasten the possibility that action might some day be taken.

A book like this is likely to be attacked, if at all, on grounds of politics. By temperament and inclination I stand on the right of the political fence. Unlike the present administration, however, of which I am nominally a supporter, I believe that discussion needs to be followed by some form of action, however minuscule.

This book is not really about political leadership, though some asides are in order and have been duly made. It is about the record of what for want of a better term, one can still call the governing classes.

Writing a book like this presents problems. It demands discussing not only the obvious, but also digging into points of what may seem like abstruse detail. I can only plead that many of the things that are wrong can only be properly observed in such details.

And this leads me to the other part of this book's origins – the Suez débâcle. What struck me then was not the questionable morality – though this too is arguable – but the near-criminal stupidity, the bungling, the incompetence and general flabbiness of what poses for leadership of one of the most complex societies ever run by man. Shortly afterwards, a journalist writing in the *Spectator* used a phrase which has ever since stuck in my mind: 'We are ruled,' he stated, 'by a collection of chancers and *après moi le déluge* men.' Nearly seven years later, one can see that things have not changed much. It is my contention that they should. It may be that people deserve the leadership they get: but I still cannot see what we have done to deserve ours.

Paris–London, May 1963

Chapter 1

The Industrial Society

Although this is a book about manufacturing industry, it is not about all parts of it equally. It is mainly concerned with the recent history of some of the more important growth industries, chiefly those which are or should be concerned with exports. It deals with much of the dismal history of the fifties and takes the view that there is only one real reason why we are in our present difficulties. It is not the fault of the trade unions, foreign competitors, nuclear pollution, the communists, or the weather. The faults lie mainly in managerial circles, particularly in the higher management areas of our major industries.

If British managerial incompetence is to blame for our difficulties, one had better state straight away, however, that it is not all the fault of industrial managers; it is also that of managers in other areas of activity: finance, education, medicine. In all spheres in which the managers can be classed as State employees – politicians, civil servants (particularly Treasury officials), etc. – they must carry the largest share of odium. For manufacturing industry does not exist in a vacuum. It is part of the society we live in and shares the same virtues, defects, and *mores*.

If then my main concern is to 'clobber' the managers, I must try to be fair and put industry within its social context, discuss the infrastructure in which it is enmeshed, and generally try to put manufacturing industry's faults into perspective. I shall try to avoid as much as possible preaching about the moral state of the nation, for this is not another State of England work. Even so, the reader will, I hope, suffer with me while I set the scene: suffer because extensive stage-setting is essential, and the resulting scene is a sombre one. Suffer also because this sort of exercise is a luxury normally denied the journalist, and I have accordingly set the stage perhaps a little exhaustively. A journalist can, I hope, then be forgiven if he takes, grasps, and generally clutches at the opportunity presented really to say what he thinks, without having to worry about editors, subs, or pressures.

'Manufacturing industry' is a vague term. In the industrially advanced countries of the west, it includes everything from shipbuilding and nuclear engineering to the manufacture of bobbysox and ladies' hairpins. This book is therefore about specific aspects and sectors of British industry: electronics, chemicals, transport manufacture – including cars and aircraft (including helicopters and other products of the defence industries) – and some parts of that loose collection of industries generally lumped together under the title 'engineering'. It is not, except in passing, about shipbuilding, most metals and basic chemicals (i.e. sulphuric acid and nitrogen), the manufacture of detergents, children's toys, and quick-frozen foods.

The lists are themselves revealing: we are discussing here the fields in which the price of the product bears little relation to its material and sales-effort content. The real costs stem from design, knowhow, processing, the wages of skilled labour forces, and plant costs, themselves governed by similar factors. The prime requisite, however, remains skills – for which men have had to serve long apprenticeships, whether on the factory floor or in universities, technical training colleges, and other academic institutions. Skilled labour forces mean labour with knowhow, not labour in terms of physical force. Thus in the case of shipbuilding the labour content is very large, but the skill content is not – at least in terms of the 1960s – for much of this labour is engaged in processes which largely consist of putting finished products together, even if they should do so using modern equipment.

There is a paradox here: the total number of skills involved in shipbuilding is in fact quite high, but the majority take place outside the shipyard. Almost any lightly industrialized country can build ships, and many of them do. What we tend to forget is that they often have a high foreign equipment content, for most countries are unable to make all the equipment required. Ship costings tend to break down into three groupings, roughly equal in value: steel, sub-deliveries, and labour. Shopping around for the first two can make costs roughly the same the world over – that this is possible, however, depends on managerial skills as well as government economic policies. When one turns to labour costs, one is governed by the national wage-patterns. In a high-cost country such as ours, management finds itself paying more for unskilled labour than many others do for skilled. Add a traditional approach to building, lack of modern handling equipment, of modern tools – both for labour and management – and a low capital investment rate, and you have the position of today: British shipyards with few exceptions largely dependent on government orders, and on the modernization and repair of ships usually flying the British flag. Otherwise one finds shipyards obtaining orders given to us for reasons other than the purely economic, that is, linked to barter deals or to our provision of the purchase money on easier terms than those given by our competitors. (This last unfortunately is a rarity.) There are of course exceptions, but, writing in general terms, the British shipbuilding industry has little knowhow which is not also in the hands of other people. More important, it cannot call on a combination of exclusive skills or in practice build as fast as many other countries. The Japanese throughput, for example, is twice as fast as the British. (This, one suspects, is owing not only to more modern equipment in its shipyards but also to the way in which many of them are organized.) The larger Japanese shipyards are not only more modern; they are also parts of larger companies dealing with materials in connected fields. The result is often that much more is made within the company than is possible here. This situation applies too in some parts of Western Europe. In Germany for example such yards as Howaldt-werke can call on the resources of A.E.G., the large electrical and engineering group in control, and does comparatively less shopping around.

But to return to the growth industries. These industries are known as growth industries for another reason, this time concerned with their markets: they are partly growth because they are export industries. Whether we like it or not in theory, in practice the limitations of lack of skilled labour and lack of capital force most of the world's underdeveloped nations into industrialization in a certain fashion – that is if they intend to industrialize at all. The start is to create a pool of skills to begin operating a basic pattern of industries, coal mining (where coal exists), electricity generation, iron and steel, textiles, and some consumer goods. These are usually linked with the development of assembling industries in the engineering fields, and some plants connected with arms manufacture. More often than not, there will also be an ore-mining industry of some kind, usually run by foreign companies. Engineering industries on the scale we think of them, however, are normally absent, and the State has to depend on foreign products for much of its basic needs. This may be partly disguised by policies designed to make foreign manufacturers at least assemble within the country concerned (as in Portugal), but it does not change the basic dependence. Many of these countries have unavoidable adverse trading balances, and as their foreign exchange becomes used up, they begin to restrict imports. It is then that their real dependence becomes more obvious (as can be seen by looking at the list of products which such countries as India have to import – dire economic straits or no). The backbone of these imports is high skill content products whose main purpose is to help to create the infrastructure of the modern state. This in its turn is expected to help these countries to do what we have done: to get on to the treadmill of rising standards of living as fast as possible.

With a population of fifty-two million, the fifth or sixth highest living-standard in the world, and no resources apart from our brains and skill, we too, however, are on a treadmill. Our living, as I hope I have shown, largely depends on being able to do what other people cannot: supplying things in short supply elsewhere at the right time, or manufacturing better quality goods than our competitors at cheaper prices. In practice this amounts to staying alive by staying ahead.

If we date the modern world as beginning at the end of the Second World War, we find the United Kingdom in a very favourable position. The physical power of its main European competitor, Germany, had been destroyed, and the United Kingdom, industrially and socially, was the most advanced country in Europe – in both real and *per capita* terms. What has happened since then? In terms of production we have been overtaken by Germany, and the rate of growth in the industrialized world is such that we may also be overtaken by France by 1970. Why?

Whatever the N.E.D.C. may predict as a growth rate for the future, the 2·4 average growth rate of the fifties is a depressingly low one. But it would be a mistake, as I stated earlier, to discuss industrial growth in isolation from the background in which industry must operate. Though in fact the relationship is much more complex than this implies, the overall climate conditions and limits growth – or helps it. The mood of the country, though not statistically measurable, is of great importance here, as is the condition of what we now call the infrastructure. So what does this look like?

What we have at present is what we may think of as the second best society, and we can perhaps illustrate this by listing some of the many varied problems which we face; not in any order of priorities but as they come to mind. Currently Britain lacks a sufficiency of dentists in private and public practice. Result? One is that the schools' dental service has become a farce. The current most reliable estimate (by which one means one made by independent sources. It is a commentary on the society we live in that few people with research experience will accept government sources as accurate, comprehensive, or reliable) is that fifty per cent of the children in Britain's State schools do not see the dentist sufficiently regularly for almost universal prevention of tooth decay among the young to be anything more than a pipe dream: this for at least one or two generations more. Just to make the situation even worse, of those who see the dentist, only about half may have the chance of treatment, and that usually no more than once a year.

The National Health Service machinery creaks. There are not enough General Practitioners, and the system by which they are paid is not conducive to their giving the best treatment possible, even if they had the time and the facilities or knew what it was. Of those we have, the number who have any knowledge of preventive medicine, or psychiatry, is pitifully small. And even where they know of either, they are under such pressure that the first is almost impossible, and there are just not enough competent psychiatrists around to whom G.P.s can send patients – even if they could recognize the symptoms. (This is of course what happens when psychiatry is allowed to fall outside the main stream of medicine.) We do not have enough nurses in hospitals, or enough qualified social workers outside them, and even if we did have there are not enough facilities for them to work with, or the money made available to pay them. There is a shortage not only of hospitals, but also of all the special after-care units to support them; and in both cases most of the buildings we have would enrage any self-respecting young architect (under forty). As if this were not enough there are few good architects over forty in the country. The best products of that generation emigrated many years ago or work overseas, and the results of their stay can be found all over South America, Asia, the Middle East, and the Antipodes.

Within the hospitals and units there is a shortage of specialists and social workers of all types. Yet the lack of correlation between the various parts of the service – particularly between the doctor and the hospital – makes it even more essential that these should not be understaffed. If any of the other State services were to be run under such pressures, the Commons would be in a constant uproar. The effects of this can be seen in the absentee rate due to illness, a burden which has to be carried largely by industry. All this results from an inability of government to correlate sufficiently the workings of the system it theoretically controls. For the public the resultant gaps mean that it does not get the service it deserves – and directly and indirectly pays for.

It is currently almost impossible to talk of mental-health facilities. A doctor of my acquaintance maintains that if you go mad the only thing to do is to emigrate out of the Anglo-Saxon world. Possibly because this is the Anglo-Saxon world, however, we have more people per thousand of the population who have mental – particularly sexual – problems than any other country in Western Europe, and our attitudes to this would not look enlightened even in the still feudal south of Italy.

On the public-health side, we are gradually being faced with a water shortage in the major connurbations, something which even the worst weather in Europe can do little to alleviate, and crash programmes may well be needed to overcome it. A large part of the public drainage system of this country is, to put it mildly, antiquated. We are, for example, still using drains in many parts of London which were first put down in the early nineteenth century. The number of local authorities using modern methods of waste disposal is small, their equipment does not largely conform to modern standards of hygiene, and even if it did, they often do not have sufficient staff to be able to provide a more than inadequate service. We do not even have enough rat-catchers or other sanitary and public-health employees; and the average public toilet is a disgrace.

If one turns to communications and the telephone – which looks like Edison's original model – we find ourselves in almost as big a mess. The telephone system is so poor that we use it less than any other industrialized nation in the world – let alone Europe. Far from the S.T.D. policy bringing in new business to the Post Office, the evidence is that it has driven business away, for according to the Post Office receipts have fallen in the areas where S.T.D. has been introduced. (The Post Office and the government too have put a dead hand on the development of radio communications by industry, preferring to retain the air space for mythical Government needs.) And never at any time since the war has the Post Office had sufficient means at its disposal to make equipment generally available to those who need it when they need it. In the field of television we have watched the public invest almost £1,000 million in receivers which will eventually have to be thrown away. It was an unnecessary investment, for the system we will be switching to was in existence at the war's end when the Cohen Committee advised the then government to continue expanding the system on 405 lines. These are not technical problems: technically there is little doubt that the electronics industry and the Post Office between them cope; indeed the Post Office has long had it in its competence to solve many of these problems. Some of the most advanced communications research in the world is done in Post Office laboratories. S.T.D., for example, was a technique which could have been introduced a quarter of a century ago. If it had been, on the then existing price structure, it is most probable that the build-up in Post Office business would have been much more satisfactory than it has been.

The man responsible for the introduction of S.T.D. was Mr Marples, who has now gone on to wreck our other means of communications: the railways. Dr Beeching's policy of wholesale railway closure seems to be in keeping with I.C.I.'s policies during the fifties and is likely to prove as ineffective. The one thing British Railways still have not learned, it seems, is cost analysis. This may seem a mundane detail; but in fact it is not. The whole of the Beeching exercise stands or falls on the analysis of costs, for it is this which dictates whether or not lines will be closed. Unfortunately the Beeching Report really discloses not only that the Chairman of British Railways does not understand the terminology, but also that he has done the wrong sums, and done them badly.

17

What's Wrong with British Industry?

The social consequences of Beeching are that people will inevitably be drawn even further into existing towns, when our need is to reduce town pressures. The way in which the policy is being carried out also gives little hope that the Government or the Railways Board understand either the technological revolution that is going on or the social consequences in the areas concerned. (With an output equivalent figure of under £900 a head, what do you expect?) And just to make matters worse, the traction system picked for the main lines gives indications that it is not necessarily the best or the cheapest. For these one has to go abroad to such countries as Sweden, Switzerland, and France. (Railway safety standards too have become so bad that I was recently advised by a railwayman to travel in the rear of expresses and the front of slow trains, on the principle that these are the safest places in accidents.) What stands out from the much praised Beeching report is its nice Victorian approach to the problems of transport. There is no mention of any of the newer and cheaper forms of fixed-line system – yet we are going to invest huge sums in 'modernizing' a system which even on completion will be roughly in the position of almost everyone else's ten years ago, thus putting even further off the date when we can have a system more in keeping with existing technical knowledge.

On the roads it seems beyond Mr Marples and his advisers to comprehend that what we need in this country is not just somewhere to drive, but also somewhere to park; that the journey in fact, providing it is tolerably fast, straightforward, and comfortable, is not really as important a part of the exercise as the arrival. The one thing that the Ministry of Transport will not face is that as the car exists at present we shall never have enough road space to fill all needs, unless we turn these islands into one gigantic sea of concrete. Though the Minister continues quite happily to coerce and try to bluff the motorist, he does not have the nerve to try the same operation on the major car manufacturers. A limitation in the size of cars to fit in with the normal passenger load would go a long way to solve the problem without tearing up even more of what is still, in many parts, a pleasant country.

It is time too that we went beyond the mechanically inefficient, wasteful, technically antiquated petrol engine; time that safety equipment was made essential on a car as part of its basic equipment – and that some incentive was given to manufacturers to make them go in this direction.

On the physical face of England there are other problems too. Local government tends to be run by retired small shopkeepers or military gentlemen, and we get, it seems, the architectural tastes of the two filling up the available space. Much of the public building going up in the country is reminiscent of the Führer's bunker or the cantonment boxes so beloved by the military in India and the former colonies. As for private building, the general rule seems to be that you can put up anything you like providing it is draughty, uncomfortable, badly lit, fitted with outside drainage, and – fake oak beams apart – reverently mock Tudor. The *Punch* jokes of the thirties on this subject could – were it not that they are perhaps not hard enough for current public taste – be printed today, and they would still be as relevant. And much of private building is a rather bad joke, much of public housing is a nightmare.

Apart from the quality of the new architecture, to clear all the slums at the present rate of progress and house everyone would take up to the year 2000 – by which time much that is currently being built will also need pulling down.

Now let us take our educational system. We have proportionately the smallest number of young people at university of any country in Europe (even including Turkey as part of Europe). After making allowance for the difference in standards between some British and American university courses, and including in the British total those who go to technical colleges and other centres of adult education, *pro rata* we still find four Americans going to university for every Briton. Even the Russians send – again *pro rata* – two to our one. It is now generally accepted that we do not get as much as half the top ten per cent of the nation's brain power into the universities, so that even on its own premises, the élite system we have geared ourselves to works only by chance, and not by design. The result is that with the outflow of quality (much of it almost immediately emigrates), we also educate a large percentage who on the present basis should not have gone to a university at all. In physical terms the universities are overloaded and the staff overworked, where departments have any staff at all. We give the highest allowances in Europe, and then make sure that there is not enough university accommodation available, so that a large number of the students will have to live out, usually in poor, overpriced accommodation. The result is that many students have to do paid work in their vacations. There is little wrong with this except of course that the vacations are really meant for academic work, and that the loss of such work has a lot to do with the semi-literacy of too many graduates. Moreover, we then proceed to set a tax-free income level for the student, so low and so geared that if he earns anything resembling the rate for the job (and possibly obtains some benefit from paid work), his parents' financial payment contributions will be increased.

When we turn to pre-university education what do we see? We know that classes are overcrowded; that we do not have enough teachers and, what is more, are unlikely to obtain them within this century; that a large number of schools in this country should be knocked down; that standards are low; and that – though no politician will ever publicly face it – for a large part of the population the school system we have is an inglorious waste of time. Through its elected representatives (usually carefully selected for it by an unrepresentative group) the public makes sure that there won't be enough teachers to go round. And in their attempts at keeping the politicians' hands off educational syllabi, people themselves pay little attention to their contents. The result is a science syllabus at least half of which could easily be thrown out without loss, history tuition which is generally a farce. (We get angry, for example, about the lack of attention paid in German schools to the Hitler and war periods. At the same time, the normal British syllabus often stops – if people are lucky enough to come so close to the present day – at 1919.) It is only the British who could be responsible for starting a society (Mensa) for intellectuals which is itself based on entrance tests long known by everyone else to be generally invalid. Is it any wonder then that the quality of British intellectual life has reached its present low?

We have politicians who mean well, but whether or not they are well equipped to carry out the tasks that need doing is a different matter. The air is thick with evasions, half-truths, and downright lies from all parts of the political spectrum. This is not generally due to any wish to mislead, for these are by and large as decent and honourable men as you are likely to find in public life under the British system. Thus the Prime Minister can see fit to tell us that we have doubled our rate of investment in ten years, and talks of no one ten years ago dreaming that we could be in the position we are in today. But to say this is to make nonsense of what every-one except politicians seems to have known was a possibility. We are faced too with Ministers harking back with nostalgia to the unnatural calm of the turn of the century and talking of ending criticism in a destructive and cynical way. (One is tempted to say that faced with Lord Hailsham and Lord Home, the public reaction is understandable.) It seems indeed beyond the wit of politicians to understand that what they hold dear and what the rest of the country really worries about are nowadays two different things. Most of the things I have quickly discussed have been creeping up on us for a long time. The immediate scene is, however, of just as much interest to those engaged in industry. During the period this book has been written, we have had man-made smog in London (something one is now unlikely to see often even in the industrial areas of the Ruhr), something which more active government intervention after the smog of 1952 should by now have ended. We have had a long, hard winter, with its power cuts due to faulty estimating of electrical demand. It gives a good idea of the strength of the statistical machinery at the government's command that the faults in the Electricity Board estimates should not have been discovered or, obviously, properly checked, even though the government at the time had to find the money for the investment. During the same winter we have seen the inability of the local and central machinery to keep the roads open, the lack of modern clearance equipment available to Local Authorities, making the situation even worse. We have watched antiquated methods – such as the laying of gravel because few people had the foresight to lay in enough salt – being used in the knowledge that when the snows shifted we should find many of the roads partly broken up, and the rate-payers stuck with the bill. We have seen a lack of correlation between public service authorities such that three or four times the necessary manpower was required to do a repair job. We have watched also the habit of mind at work which refuses to pay overtime for a job to be done at a week-end, resulting in transport delays during the week, the cost of which is paid by both industry and the public. All this on top of normal road de-lays currently thought to cost us some hundreds of millions of pounds.

How did we get into this state? The answer is twofold. First, the extremely low intellectual standards we set for men in public life. It could be argued of course that the reason we remain a free country is that we are in such a mess. As things stand, a *coup d'état* is not only undesirable, it is also impossible! The men may be available, but they are not in politics.

This is yet but a small selection of the problems which face us. We have others: the law, now more of a 'hass' than ever as the odds on obtaining justice lengthen every year. The relationship of the government to industry: when no industrialist can rely absolutely on the honesty of the government and the machinery of the State, he must take measures to protect his interests and those of his shareholders. This among other measures means charging cost plus, which in turn can have a deleterious effect on industrial health (as will become apparent when we come to deal with the aircraft industry). In these and many other departments of the nation's life we need not just a drastic overhaul, but a wholesale re-casting.

But we must draw a line somewhere, so let us draw it now and return to our theme. Do these things affect industry, and if so how? Take first our educational system and its industrial effect. We have constructed a system where the ponderous is taken to be the knowledgeable and the authoritative. Few people, however, are naturally inclined in this direction. The result? Something never publicly admitted (except by inference): tens of thousands of youngsters are every year thrown on to a labour market for which they are educationally unfitted. We have over the past decade had possibly the highest true illiteracy rate in Western Europe (I do not count Spain or Portugal as part of Western Europe); the highest rate that can be attributed to the system's failure to educate those in its grasp (not the highest overall, simply because elsewhere they stand more chance of getting away).

Now what happens next? The ever-growing demand is for skilled men; to become skilled, however, men must be trained. This means both a sufficiency of applicants with enough basic knowledge to be trained, and enough places for them to obtain their training. Many employers say quite frankly that though the educational standards may have risen, they have not risen fast enough or covered enough people to be able to cope with the demand for youngsters suitable for training. Hence at the training level we always have a skilled labour gap. This error is further compounded by an archaic apprentice system, the lack in any case of enough apprenticeship facilities within firms, and the until now even more depressing lack of national standards and their enforcement. We are beginning to do something about this, but that we should have to wait until 1963 for some sort of national approach to these problems is a good illustration of the lack of activity that is the chief characteristic of the post-war period. (The Germans, to pick but one example, have had a system generally better than this since the 1920s.) Good apprenticeship facilities do of course exist; but as they are organized on a company basis, and roughly one firm in 200 in this country has over 1,000 employees, while more than two thirds do not reach double figures, the company incentives to train workers and opportunities that are lost are considerable. Few small employers train skilled workers: they let the large companies do this – and then poach.

If we turn to the field of higher education, we find ourselves in a peculiar position. We are the only country in Europe which believes it is possible academically to train engineers in three years: everyone else takes longer. And even with this short period of training we do not get enough of them. There is a great deal in the two cultures argument and the theory of the dominance of almost everything by men untrained in the sciences and technologies. It ignores, however, the lack of highly trained people available generally and the unsuitability of too many engineers for higher posts largely because too short an academic training has meant too narrow a background. This is no fault of the people concerned, these are simply the facilities we offer. (Even so, this is not always a handicap for scientists and technologists, as we shall discuss. Any training is, after all, better than none.)

We lack not only engineers, however, we lack specialists of all kinds. Why? We face another handicap besides our inability to get more than half the people into universities who should be there. Even for those who do go, the structure is so unbalanced that we cannot obtain enough of the scientists, mathematicians, statisticians, and other specialists we need to man our industrial machine, even if, that is, industry were keyed to use them. It is here that the so-called brain drain to the United States becomes even more serious than its small numbers imply. This general shortage has all sorts of effects. It is not news that we have been one of the slowest countries in Europe to make use of computers (even though we had more computer companies than the rest of Western Europe put together during most of the last ten years).

What's Wrong with British Industry?

One side of the business which has collapsed almost entirely, at least under British management, is the field of analogue computers. Now analogue units have considerable uses in industry. At the analogue-computer level, however, the two main companies are now both American-owned (American companies abroad are notoriously long-sighted). Why then are analogue computers only slowly introduced into industry? For a start, they are only of limited applications, with government departments and large industrial units as the main customers. This is not the sole reason, however. To get the best out of analogue computers you need good mathematicians. These are available only just in sufficient numbers to fill the growing university demand; and we know that industry as currently organized is for the majority the last possible place they would go to for work. This emerges from surveys and from the ill-starred attempts of companies to lure them into industry

What is true of the best of our university output of mathematicians is also applicable to many other areas of the sciences. Outside London, industry even has problems obtaining the services of able economists: many try industry and then pass on either to the city or back to academic life.

Let us now turn to some other effects of the State machine on industry. It is a commonplace that our costs are high. They are high not only because output stubbornly refuses to grow in line with costs, or because we do not work as hard as the French, the Germans, or even the industrial workers of Lichtenstein, but also because our service costs are high. The constant loading of cost of the power stations of the future on to the paying customers of today, for example, means that at the same time as electricity consumption is rising, a growing number of companies are installing their own generation equipment, finding it cheaper to provide their own power than to buy it from the Central Electricity Generating Board.

We have discussed too the S.T.D. system. The recently introduced higher trunk charges are due largely to Post Office miscalculations of the revenue the original tariff would bring in. What little evidence has been available shows that some businesses – particularly banks – were beginning to use the telephone much more because it paid them to do so. Instead of effectively publicizing the charges, however, the Post Office did very little to try to increase business.

Instead, after a relatively short period, they put the charges up again. Result? I have met quite a few people who are beginning to take a much more serious look at their mounting telephone bills – and are thinking in terms of the economies they may have to make.

Think if you will of one or two industrial problems created by our now not so glamorous welfare state machinery. The only side we have covered more fully than the Germans or the French is the medical. If you want equitable pensions, guaranteed holidays with pay, family allowances, or efficient and humane subsidiary medical services (that is, those not covered by the general practitioner, the hospitals, and the pharmacies), you have again to go to the Continent. On the pension side the meagreness of the State pension is such that everyone who can has contracted out. Side by side with this there has grown up a crazy patchwork quilt of private schemes. The result now is that the pension a man will obtain is not governed by length of service, standards of equity, his job, or the contributions he pays, but by the availability of pension schemes operated by firms in his area, and their contributions to them. The difficulties in the way of pension transfers are considerable, thus hindering the mobility of labour. In the field of health we have a long way to go. There are probably twice as many (or three or four, or five times as many, for no one knows) working days lost in the year through illnesses and visits to the doctor and the specialist as there are through strikes. Illnesses happen, one has to accept this; but has anyone any idea of the amount of time wasted hanging around in hospital waiting rooms to cure these ills? Complaints of lost time are heard, up and down the country. How many man-hours are lost here simply because there is hardly a hospital in the country in which the directing staff have as much idea of organization as is found even in the most backward business?

Everywhere we turn the machinery creaks. In the field of transport we know that something like five per cent of the road system takes nearly two thirds of the traffic. The consequent delays are familiar to every road user. That traffic cannot flow freely means for example that extra transport must be maintained by firms, as must extra staff, thus swelling many companies' fleets, and their costs, all of which of course must eventually be paid for by someone. I have written earlier that this costs hundreds of millions, and this may well be true. How many, however, no one can say with any real accuracy – the position we find ourselves in with many other problems. It will have become obvious by now that too many of the effects of the machinery we as a society live in are unknown.

Much of the time the only judgements we can make are that these things do have an effect, and an adverse one. There are many other things we do not know, and one awaits the census of production figures with interest. (After all we are still using the 1951 figures!) But even when the new complete figures come along, they will be out of date, and not really comprehensive, for the government, because of many deficiencies in the statistical machinery, will still not know exactly what we made and who made it. Thus planning in any but the broadest sense becomes almost meaningless. Given these almost ancient problems it can be seen that the modernization of our society is going to be a slow, long job.

Where, if anywhere, have we gone wrong? I would nominate as the central issue the 'Them–Us' problem – which is in any case no new thing, for from it have sprung the trade unions and the Labour Party. From it, too, springs the feeling of insecurity of much of the population, the determination not to work oneself out of a job, even though that job may be as obsolescent and as powerless as the T.U.C. General Council. It is true of course that the British do not work as hard as their European competitors. There is generally little encouragement to do so. In almost any West German industry, you find people working harder when they are at work. But then they have as a matter of course twelve days off a year for religious and other festivals, three weeks' paid holidays, and more job security.

This blanket of condemnation is in fact full of holes. If we look carefully at industry we can spot many examples of companies both large and small where security exists, working conditions are better than the norm, and productivity is comparatively high. Again and again one is struck by one of two things: either the companies are controlled by people with shop-floor experience who understand what makes them tick, or else they are controlled by foreigners – usually American. A New York executive I know says that if he were asked to give advice to American youngsters who dislike their local rat race, yet still want to forge ahead without too much effort, he would simply advise him: join an American company which operates abroad, and go East, young man!

Chapter 2

Whose Industrial Problem?

The tenor of this work will by now have become apparent. Its central theme is that we have really only one basic problem, that of management of limited resources and skills. Other problems may and do exist, but they are all subsidiary ones, and we should remember this to save ourselves being sidetracked. Some of course are spurious – for example, the problem of strikes (we have fewer strikes per worker than the Americans, but no one thinks America is collapsing). The loss of six million work days last year is not even equivalent to the time lost by one week's tea-breaks across the working population. (Not that one has any wish to cut down tea-breaks, which modern techniques show can have a considerable beneficial effect on increased concentration, well-being, and production in many otherwise monotonous industrial jobs.) Indeed the arguments about tea-breaks (with workers and sociologists for and some managements against) that still periodically crop up in industry provide us with our first clue about the managerial problems. Arguments against tea-breaks and the evidence are the sort of thing which would be more in keeping with the more highly 'Them–Us' class warfare charged conditions which still existed before the Second World War and which I discussed earlier. In current conditions they are even more of an irrelevance. Why, then, do they crop up?

They are relics of an earlier tradition, the misnamed amateur tradition. An amateur in the past was someone who could financially afford to be so. The workers (this term is currently also a misnomer. I use it because it forms a mental image which, hackneyed though it is, almost everyone understands) had no time, they were too busy earning a living. The real point about the amateur tradition, which we have now debased to mean that a man with a

27

ucation from the right schools is fit for anything, is that it bore little relation to the tradition as we know it now. It was of limited importance in industry, which in any case was beyond the pale for all but the most securely socially established and the eccentric. Where the amateur classes did impinge on the industrial world, they did so in the same thorough fashion as they pursued their other overriding passions, with an interest which if not legally recognizable as professional, was in fact its equivalent. They (or we – take your pick) might not be seen trying in public, this did not go with the tradition, but a lot went on in private. This part of the tradition is unfortunately no longer with us. What we now have is the rubbish of the inexpert in all fields, the socially acceptable all-rounder.

It is of course felt at its strongest in the old middle class, who can remember what were for them (though not necessarily for anyone else) better days. The industrial society we live in is not simply one manufacturing largely old-style products, it is one also largely run by old men, or men brought up among the half-remembered remnants of an older tradition – one not particularly well fitted to survive or otherwise it would have given more evidence of being able to master present-day conditions. Now old age is not a crime – in any case some of the oldest men I know are still in their twenties. Neither is it a crime to seek the familiar; what is perhaps dangerous is to leave power in the hands of people to whom the familiar is the unreal, the no longer existent. It shows itself not only in the emulation of the near illiterate, semi-agricultural aristocracy – another shorthand term – but also in grasping at other familiar things. The manufacture of familiar products, a resistance to change in both ideas and production, the organization of business on lines which would have been approved of by our grandfathers, a concentration on the known parts of the business process, such as comparatively small-scale production, and the 'where there's muck there's money' approach to business which created the ugliness of many of our industrial towns.

All these things tend to create a top managerial class conservative in the extreme. It is conservative in a special sense. While it may make use of the specialist services which modern industries need (though the little evidence available suggests that it generally does not do so) it is seldom happy in the same fashion as its juniors. Thus for example in another sphere neither De Gaulle, Macmillan, nor Adenauer managed their affairs with the same observable enthusiasm or the same assurance as Kennedy who was at home in the sixties, not just as a professional in a professional's world, but simply because this was his world and he neither knew nor regretted the loss of another.

What characterizes our leadership, then, is a sense of uneasiness: and uneasiness breeds further doubt. It is this feeling which is observable throughout much of the top management of industry, and it is noticeable how closely it is linked to age. Can one in fact bracket old age and amateurism, and produce as a result this general feeling? There are old amateurs (in the strict sense that they do not hold professional or other qualifications) in British industry directing companies with evident skill, enjoyment, and enthusiasm. There are younger amateurs doing the same thing. In either case one usually finds that they know their business and industry extremely thoroughly and are really professionals. Professionalism after all is unlikely ever to be restricted to men with university degrees – even if they are in the right subjects. There are exceptions to every rule – particularly in business.

Thorn, of Thorn Electrical Industries (who has possibly a wider knowledge of his competitors' costs at his fingertips than anyone else in any sector of industry); Sir Leon Bagrit of Elliott Automation: these are but two names from a short list of men running large companies with considerable éclat, efficiency, and both long- and short-term profit (even if on the stock market those profits have usually been discounted years ahead by investors seeking a good thing) and without the sort of background which an ordered society would expect. It is noticeable that only one of these names – the second – should be widely known to the public. These men are the non-joiners to whom business is an almost full-time occupation. One has the impression that they make the right noises in public only because a certain amount is expected of them, that they are in fact much happier back in the factory, office, or development laboratory.

Professionalism then is not really a matter of age, it is largely a matter of attitudes and aptitudes. The names I have used above, however, though not hand picked, are revealing. These are men running two of the successes of British industry. Can one in fact establish a causal link between professionalism in its widest sense and success? I think one can, and I hope I may be forgiven for approaching it in a somewhat roundabout fashion. (What I write here also may be taken to be self evident. It is a mark of the mess we are in that the evidence on the subject is either subjective or allows only inferential comparisons – for the ground work just has not been done.)

Management of industry, in the sense in which our competitors talk of it – by which one means purposeful management – is as yet a fragile new thing in Britain. It is no accident that the few able industrial leaders we have are usually the first people on record as being in favour of some form of management training. That Company x is headed by a genius says something about its chance of survival *now*; it says little about its chance of survival in the future, for one cannot postulate a company's continued existence and prosperity on the chance that one genius will automatically be succeeded by another. Indeed the position is usually the reverse as geniuses tend to be surrrounded by either dwarfs or yes-men. But before we return to the equation professionalism $=$ success (to which in this world there are of course also always exceptions), we must try to decide what management is.

It is symptomatic of our current state of muddle-headedness that its definitions should bear little relationship to what is actually going on. Thus the first entry under management in my *Concise Oxford Dictionary* is concerned with management in its least important, most archaic verbal sense: management as 'trickery, deceitful contrivance'. Neither is there much help to be found in industry or the Institutes, for no real definition of management exists which is acceptable to everyone. Some people fall back on that guide to company market activity, the old first law of business, which is to maximize profits. (Berthold Beitz, Chairman of the West German steel and engineering giant Fried. Krupp, also holds this view, but then goes on to add that it is in any case indissolubly linked to what you do with the profits you have made, and that the maximization of profit is not a simple law, but one bound by a wide complex of social, political, and economic factors, of which the social are the most important.) And, of course, if the profit/loss record is to be the industrial managerial guide, one must cease to think of the aircraft industry, and some others, as parts of the normal industrial economic scene at all, for the figures here are representative not only of company effort, but national effort in the form of taxpayers' subventions. Thus we have no general managerial guide to management, and we cannot agree on what it is, though we can agree that it too must use tools: market research, operational research, economic analysis, etc., and make efforts (too often small-scale) to teach their importance. Hence we have no managerial training schools of the status of America's Harvard Business School, or M.I.T., or Zürich's Technische Hochschule; we have instead the British Institute of Management, the Administrative Staff College, and an unfortunately low-status diploma from the Regent Street Polytechnic. Can we in fact teach management when we cannot find a generally acceptable definition? But the two American institutions are in the same boat (and these two form the apex of a large pyramid of not so well known academic institutions also involved in managerial studies), yet they manage most successfully. This argument – what is management? – has bedevilled and needlessly sidetracked managerial studies for years. One arrives at the point where one asks whether it is necessary to be able to define a subject in two lines before admitting that it exists? As every child knows, no one expects an electrician to be able to define electricity.

This is not, however, the real reason why we do not as yet academically train our managers. Concurrent with the argument about management itself and what it is, there is another argument proceeding about *who* is a manager. This argument, like the silly season, is always with us, and it is concerned with the position of directors. Its most recent manifestation was the outcry when Sir Leon Bagrit replaced four part-time directors with promoted executives. The outcry of course, was led by the Institute of Directors (which it is important to realize really represents nothing except itself). The industrialist's real pressure organizations are the Federation of British Industries and the industrial societies and associations. The Institute represents directors who are not a homogeneous body or themselves an interest in the same way as are trade unions. It is unlikely that the withdrawal of labour by the Council of the Institute of Directors would have any effect at all on industry or the country. This is a great pity, for there is room in this country for a strong managerial club or organization – which the Institute is not.

'We deplore', said Sir Richard Powell, the Institute's Director General, to the *Evening Standard*, 'the overloading of boardrooms with technicians. They often can't see the wood for the trees.' (It is amusing to watch unessential organizations clothe themselves with the panoply of real power names elsewhere representing real authority. The Institute's employees do not even number one hundred, and it is doubtful if anyone is empowered to do more than speak for the council.)

With this one returns with a vengeance to our equation: the causal relationship between professionalism and success. It can be argued (and that in truth is what I am doing) that the reverse of the views of Sir Richard Powell is true: that in fact it is the professionals who see the wood, the rest who see only the trees. The post-war successes of British industry are themselves led either by boy wonders or by boards consisting mainly of technicians (even though they may be balancing acts between technicians from within the industry, technicians from the sales area of commerce, technicians from the world of finance, and technicians operating with skilled external financial advice). This is not just a local tendency, it is a world-wide one, wherever public companies form a part of the industrial scene. There is, of course, still no substitute for ownership as a way of getting to the top, but given that this is not practicable, the road to success almost everywhere else (and now fortunately increasingly so here) goes through some form of expertise. The experts can of course be as wrong as anyone else – the history of I.C.I. in the 1950s is a case in point, though here again it is fair to say that only the mixture of expertise was wrong, and that what I.C.I. needed was commercial men able to reverse the usual scientist in commerce's method of starting with a conclusion then trying to sell it without paying attention to the facts of market life.

Here again we meet a complication. I have written that we lack managerial training facilities, and inferred that too much of industry is run by amateurs. Even were conditions different there is still no guarantee that with a high-powered programme of managerial training facilities, and with the ex-trainees in the right places, we would do any better. Because in fact managerial studies are not necessarily a better guarantee of success than are operations on the current old-boy network. If they are established on the right basis, these can be as successful as any other system – and in their turn may form an old-boy net of their own. The right basis, however, needs to be more rational than the accident that is money. Indeed, in societies such as our own, academic managerial training schools are an essential. They are a replacement for the disciplines elsewhere followed as a matter of course before a man goes into business or industry.

The phenomenon that has been industrial France in the last few years has been built up without managerial training schools (though they do have one extremely good one in the not strictly French European School at Fontainebleau. It has been operating only a short time and its products have not as yet progressed far up the industrial management scale). West Germany, a country also without much in the way of management-training facilities, had a Gross National Product less than two thirds the size of that of the United Kingdom in 1950. Yet by 1961 the West German G.N.P. was bigger than the British. If management is such a skilled occupation that it requires higher educational establishments, how then have these two countries accomplished this growth? Indeed why is it that the growth rates across a wider cross section of nations for the years 1950–60 are as in the table below, with Britain, as is now becoming shamingly almost traditional, at the bottom.

G.N.P. *compound growth rate* – 1950–60

Germany	7·6
Italy	5·9
Netherlands	4·9
Switzerland	4·9
France	4·3
Sweden	3·3
U.S.A.	3·3
Belgium	2·8
U.K.	2·4

If one must make comparisons it is perhaps best, however, to restrict them mainly to comparisons with West Germany and France, countries with industries which are in many ways of similar complexity, and with similar problems to our own.

The first significant fact we come across is the, by our standards, extreme professionalization of management in both countries. The methods of achievement of course differ, but their effect is the same. Until now in Germany management professionalization has been achieved by competition (this works here too. One has only to look at some of our industries which are constantly exposed to competition from abroad. At its top levels the oil industry is modern, efficient, and, even with bureaucratic habits, well run. Much of the City's financial machinery, particularly in insurance, is extremely skilfully operated, and there are some smaller industries where in a present-day European context we have little to learn). So, in a country of high skill industries, at top levels only the able survive – and they do so partly by a willingness to accept that technicians of all kinds have a place in top management.

In Germany it goes much further than this: the 'Dr Eng.', with his long academic training, is himself within the management tradition. The firm's owner does not send his son to university to do a B.A. in almost anything considered the arts side of education; he sends him to do engineering, as he has done almost since industry in the modern sense began. And if one thinks in terms of the social model, it has never been the social disgrace that it is here to come up through the technical side of the Armed Services. It has not been the dimwits who go on to Service technical schools, it is the career men. The dimwits and social career officers stayed in the regiments.

The French approach is a different one. France, it is now being generally acknowledged, is run by an old-boy net. If there were old school ties one would discover that the men manning the key positions in the State, the services – armed and public – and the larger units of industry were all from the same schools. The factor which determines whether or not they go to these schools (the *grandes écoles*), however, is not just money and social position – though these can play a part in that as elsewhere it is the moneyed families and the middle classes who are determined that their children will do well. The main factor determining entrance is intelligence. And what are these schools? At the apex of the pyramid stands the Polytéchnique, a school founded by Napoleon to provide the army with technically trained officers. The programme here is loaded with the formal maths and science disciplines. It is from this school particularly that the French 'mandarinate' stems. And the competitive examinations which decide whether or not one goes to the Polytéchnique are themselves only open to *baccalauréat* (equivalent to G.C.E. A level, though the standard is in fact much higher) successes with high enough marks. As the school is an Army institution, the candidates have also to be physically fit. The results of this selection and training are apparent all over France. As Polytéchniciens have undergone the same thorough basic academic training, communication between them is possible in the sense that it may not be here with men from different disciplines. This has a telling effect on French life. Though the majority may be in government service, this, now that the French no longer have an empire, is not big enough to cope with them all; and so they are found in all the major branches of French industrial life, particularly in the major French companies in the growth fields. Planning and logic (though the French are a most illogical people) comes naturally to ex-students brought up on Cartesian logic and its mathematical tools, and France has once again been rebuilt accordingly. This is not the competitive (or short term cooperative) exercise on which West Germany has been rebuilt. It has, however, worked, and it has worked again largely because much of the country's real élite is involved in it.

The results produced by both systems have led to talk of economic miracles. It has been easier to say this than to face the twin embarrassing truths that, in these two countries, both management and labour *work*, and that for any industrial system to do so, it must be wedded to some sort of reasonably comprehensible philosophy. In Britain we talk of a mixed economy, evidently believing that the bold statement will excuse the lack of thought that still orders our affairs. In fact, almost everyone else's is a mixed economy – even if the pattern of government control over the parts of the economy in which it wishes to have a say differs from country to country.

Whatever the system followed, the effects in both countries have proved staggering, expressed either in the growth rate percentage increase terms shown earlier, or in index or cash terms. If we take the G.N.P. index as standing at 100 in 1950, by 1960 it stood at 205 in West Germany, 150 in France, and 125 in the United Kingdom. If we take the growth in G.N.P. in cash terms we can observe (see table on next page) that, if the British economy had grown by the same ratios as in either West Germany or France, we should have said a permanent good-bye to economic crises long before the fifties were over.

Even had we grown at the French rate, the annual British product would still have been worth over £5,000 million a year more by 1960. Presuming that exports of manufactured goods had increased within the same ratio, the increase in our annual exports at the start of the sixties would have been around £800 million a year.

What's Wrong with British Industry?

Growth in G.N.P. – $ 1,000 million to nearest 1,000 ·

	West Germany	France	U.K.
1950	33,000	38,000	56,000
1960	69,000	58,000	71,000

Growth in U.K. G.N.P. had West German or French growth rates been possible

If West Germany's 6·1 per cent mean annual rate had applied to the U.K.	1950 1960	56,000 106,000
If France's 4·3 per cent growth rate had applied to the U.K.	1950 1960	56,000 85,000

But of course, they did not. Indeed not only has our G.N.P. stubbornly refused to grow at a rate comparable with that of the other industrialized countries, our exports too have shown a tendency to fall both as a percentage of world exports (this is a further pointer to the soundness of Professor Barna's thesis, for about three-quarters of the world's export trade in manufactured goods is in those with a high skill content) and in comparison with many other countries. Thus by 1960, while our exports were equivalent to about one sixth of our G.N.P., having fallen from nearly one fifth, West Germany's had grown from less than one sixth to nearly a quarter. Social attitudes and government policies apart, are there any clear reasons ascribable to management why this should be so?

There are a number, and they are readily identifiable. It is currently axiomatic that, given more capital investment by industry, output would increase. This is the view that Mr Macmillan evidently shares. It can be described simply as rubbish, for our capital investment is already higher than most countries. I write this during the farce that is National Productivity Year. A study made by a firm of management engineers in 1962 showed that many leading American, European, and Japanese companies are obtaining at least twice the amount of sales per person employed as are their British equivalents. In the case of America, this is so even though the employed assets of the companies concerned rose over the six years studied by only sixteen per cent, whereas in Britain they rose by nearly eighty per cent. It may be true that though our investment rate is high, it needs to be even higher. It is perhaps more true that our existing assets are under-utilized: that other people get more return for their money.

This has had a marked effect on our export prices. A country with the same wage and other cost levels but with much larger output from equivalent assets can more easily afford and absorb the *fracas* that results when trade unions make wage-increase or other demands. Where has the money gone? (It certainly has not been absorbed in wage increases. Across the industrialized world, there is a marked similarity in the amount of G.N.P. taken up by wages and salaries. Almost everywhere it is around forty per cent.)

It has been largely absorbed in other manufacturing costs. We are still bedevilled here by a quaint notion that if investment is high enough all problems will be solved. This provides solace for many of those who think it is too low, which is true. It is not only the amount of investment that is important, however, but its make-up and quality. The small-scale plant (the possibilities are as yet not very large for there are fewer than 200 firms with more than 5,000 employees in the country) which make up the bulk of this country's industrial capacity, and the hardly larger workshops which constitute the bulk of even our larger firms, have mostly been modernized. One is struck time and again, however, by the smallness of the plant installed. The more companies diversify (and the almost lunatic economic conditions of the post-war years have made this essential and attractive) the more they spread instead of concentrating resources.

But even with a wholesale programme of company rationalization and planned concentration, it is unlikely that we should be out of the wood. What we need to step up the growth rate is a concentrated programme of investment in certain industries. This can be achieved within the context of a predominantly private industry economy. Given coherent, sensible, and humane resettlement, retraining, and pension programmes, there is no reason why a considerable number of industries should not be allowed to go to the wall much faster. We need to stop the farce of Lancashire's cotton industry modernization programme happening to other industries. There is no reason why we should not have small modern industries producing high skill and capital investment content products. But there is no real need for us to do things which other people do as well and much cheaper except in so far as these industries supply local home markets, and we are content to accept their absence from the export scene, as we do already in many consumer fields.

The connexion between investment concentration and growth shows up well if one again examines such countries as France, where, though investment has over the years been much smaller than here, yet the returns have been much higher. Nor need a high rate of investment necessarily be concerned directly with production. Sweden has had a high level of investment for many years, yet the Swedish growth rate is not a high one, largely because much of that investment goes into not directly productive facilities, and because the Swedes too have mainly small-scale industries. Being in many ways the Americans of Europe, without their commitments, the Swedes can afford this much better than we. The Swedes do not, however, operate in the same climate of opinion. To innovate is respectable, for everyone understands that their future depends on it, much in the same way as to be conservative is respectable here.

So far we have spoken in terms of a low overall average growth rate and mentioned the need for concentration of investment. Within these low figures, however, a lot is happening. Some industries are growing faster than others, and some companies are doing the same, though there is not necessarily any direct connexion between the two. When dealing with companies we must distinguish between two kinds of growth: growth proper as a result of the efficient use of technical resources, and growth by merger and company rationalization. In the second, whether the purchase is done from own resources, by new issues, or by a bank loan, it is largely a reorganization programme and contributes little if anything more to the national wealth, though the new owners may have ideas of expansion in mind for the business they have bought.

There is, however, only one sound reason for a merger or takeover: to make better use of the assets than the existing management. In our present situation, it is usually only this last which is to be welcomed. What we need are more horizontal mergers, not less. Instead what we have been seeing have been attempts to merge vertically, or to diversify (we shall come to this again later).

Though these activities may in the short term be welcomed, one often has considerable doubts on the quality of the management decision involved. The short-term following of profit in unrelated fields taking advantage of what may be no more than a temporary market opportunity often does no more in the long term than give a hostage to fortune. If the companies grow, a group may eventually find itself with heavy capital demands coming from many unrelated companies with interests right across industry. In many of these fields the companies' chances of keeping up with the leaders of their sector of industry will be diminished, and the group management will be faced with many problems; problems of capital, research, production, and organization. The 1958 Census of Production points out that it is the large companies which diversify in this sense. What we are seeing, however, is not vertical or horizontal integration – both of which might make long-term economic sense. (No one should be scared of these terms. The first refers to a company or group controlling all the stages of manufacture of its product, and most if not all of those of its sale. The second means that a company or group will make a range of closely related products, or even all the sizes and permutations of one, and will restrict its activities to those particular fields of activity in which it will expect a large share of the market. It can, of course, lead to monopoly.) Instead they spread out in all sorts of unlikely activities. Fisons, for example, are engaged in the manufacture not only of a wide range of fertilizers and agricultural chemicals, but also in industrial chemicals, pharmaceuticals, veterinary pharmaceuticals, shampoos, milk, tinned foods – including hamburgers with onions – scientific apparatus, and bricks. Some of these companies are of course logical extensions of other interests. It has led, however, to a low growth rate in some parts of the group's activities, even though many of their subsidiaries' competitors are growing much faster – especially in pharmaceuticals.

This pattern, or lack of pattern, is relatively common within the large groups, and is found right across industry, again particularly within the large engineering enterprises. We have a deadly fear of monopoly here which is not in fact warranted by the facts. Given some external competition, monopolies themselves are unimportant (both in practice and in principle) in a country as small as this. What is more important is to see that monopoly power where it exists is not abused, and that inter-company or trade agreements are not used against the public interest, however the government of the time may so define it. This calls for stronger policing operations, something we shall discuss in our last chapter. The only thing left to write here is that most of the abuses of monopoly power do not in fact stem from anti-social positions. They happen because managements are lazy, have not done their homework properly in the past, and now find themselves in difficulties, or simply want a quiet life.

This is part of life at the boardroom level. There is little evidence – by which I mean I cannot find any in public print – on whether or not firms headed largely by part-time non-executive directors are the quiet lifers or not. Certainly the little digging I have done (and I put this forward most tentatively for there are, as I have indicated, some glaring examples of the reverse – the glass industry among them) indicates that what one could call abuses of monopoly power or market and price agreements within a sector of industry do occur more frequently when companies are overseen by non-executive boards, particularly those where directors have many other directorships and 'responsibilities'.

It will by now have become clear that I am a strong supporter of professional, near full-time boards of directors with managerial responsibilities. No one would deny that there is a definite need for the outside expert director; the problem arises when, as is the common practice here, there is only one board. The place for amiable nonentities, ex civil servants, or distinguished ex-soldiers is not really on a working board at all. It is on what is known in Germany as a Supervisory Board where they cannot do much harm.

We can say something else of large firms run by full-time directors as against those run on other lines. The former tend to employ more experts, and to rely more on their advice. This happens (though again my evidence is largely based on the experiences of 'experts' who have worked in industry), one suspects, for a simple reason. A full-time director, particularly a professionally trained one who has been an executive, has some conception of the training it takes to produce specialist expertise. He is attuned to taking advice and, perhaps more important, will make sure that enough of it is on tap within his organization. This applies not only to services provided within his organization, but also to those for which the firm has to go outside. Anyone who has ever studied – however slightly – any of the independent market research organizations will have been struck time and again by the types of firms which use them. They are the engineer dominated companies, or those run by salesmen. I have made my own list of one market research company's major clients: over ninety per cent of the business came from companies which were controlled by what I have been calling professionals.

It may be thought that these strictures on top management are harsh ones, and that I am alone in my complaint. In fact this is not the case; another survey published early in 1963 was one carried out of its members by the Institute of Works Managers in 1962. In nearly 500 replies, except in two of the regions, hardly anyone mentioned strikes. Their major conclusion was that top management in industry is not of the right quality. One of their most interesting deductions was that we lack cost information, but they did not go so far as to point out that though we have more than 60,000 qualified professional accountants in the country only 15,000 are qualified cost and works accountants. They made the point that there was not enough standardization, and that production runs were too often too short. (We have seen why in our quick look at the make up of industry earlier in this chapter.)

We cannot as yet leave the problems created by short-run non-standard production. The effects are felt in all sorts of likely and unlikely places. There is the effect on profit margins. Dividends are still paid, though they may not have been earned. Rather than cut the dividend, too many firms will try to make economies elsewhere, usually in their investment programme. Nor is it just the amount of investment which suffers, for as we have pointed out investment here has been high (around 2,000 companies used as a material source in one government publication have on average increased their assets two and a half times since 1950). It is in the quality of the investment.

One of the indices of figures we use to look at the state of health of industry is that concerned with machine-tool demands. We should do much better to ask ourselves 'What sort of machine tools?' Industry is certainly being re-equipped, but what with? Too much of machine-tool demand is still concentrated in manual equipment with which our forefathers would have been most at home, though it may have been titivated to look like something befitting the sixties. One has only to talk to the manufacturers of the tools of the sixties to hear of the problems that they have, not just to sell but to raise home interest in the many complex tools which should have been going into factories in the last few years.

What's Wrong with British Industry?

But no, unlike our competitors we seek the familiar. Though the bulk of our machine-tool exports are in the not-too-specialized fields, the manufacturers of complex machine tools do not report the same sales resistance to their products abroad.

Much of this chapter has been concerned not only with argument, but also with the linking of facts, of what we know but do not usually try to relate, so that most of us remain in the Chairman's fogbound maze. It should by now have become obvious that our performance is at its mildest distressing, or as Mr Harold Wincott put it in a recent *Financial Times* article, 'All I can say is that if Mr Khrushchev had been running this country since 1950 instead of Lord Attlee, Sir Winston Churchill, Lord Avon, and Mr Macmillan, the Institute of Directors would now be living in Stornoway instead of Belgrave Square.' What has happened in the major growth sectors of British industry? Let me begin with the one sector least dependent on the whims and graces of the government of the day. . . .

Chapter 3

Chemicals: The Failure of Scientific Management

The overall performance of the British chemical industry during the 1950s was, by the standards of the rest of British industry, a remarkable one. Chemical production during the period increased by nearly ninety per cent, the expansion rate during the second half of this period being around six per cent a year. This was a rate equalled only by the electrical engineering – where most of the steam was provided by electronics – and car industries.

This is impressive: or is it? During the same period, chemical production in the Common Market countries grew by well over 200 per cent. Much of our achievement too is not really chemical at all, for the industry, according to the 1958 Census of Production, is the most widely diversified in the country with considerable interests in paper, metals, engineering, and food, and it is in these fields (when seen in company and not production terms) that the industry has been making its most rapid advances. Even where it is still doing things which can be counted as chemical, however, the industry's productivity is lower than that of its American or European counterparts. The Du Ponts of this world can still manage to show double the sales value for each person employed, or two to three times the profit when expressed in terms of percentage of assets employed.

To discover how we got into this position we must take a brief look at the record of that monolith, I.C.I. Imperial Chemical Industries are Britain's and Europe's largest chemical company. At home, they account for about a quarter of the total output of the chemical industry, and within this about three fifths of the country's output of basic chemicals. This means simply that if you wish to buy British, the odds are that you will be partly buying I.C.I.

The hallmark of I.C.I. since the war, one assiduously put about by itself and its friends, was that I.C.I. is scientifically run, the emphasis being that this in itself is 'a good thing'. But if being scientific is being right, then I.C.I. was not really run scientifically, for time and again the company has been commercially as wrong as it could be. From this one infers that there was a lack of balance in I.C.I. management. The scientists' refuge that I.C.I. became may have been welcomed by the men concerned. But the I.C.I. Boards were not turned into a comparable haven for commercial experts and expertise. There was of course, no real need. I.C.I. generally led a sheltered life, operated in a heavily protected market, and could deal with imports of cheaper chemicals by some of its privately dissatisfied customers simply by complaining that this undercutting was dumping (though one senior I.C.I. man is on record as saying that no world chemical company exports at realistic prices, they all dump; I.C.I. was as guilty as the rest), and invoking mystical defence requirements in its favour. As there has never been a Conservative government unresponsive to this claim, the government always responded and put a duty on the offending imports. I.C.I. indeed played this game so frequently that cynics in the business began to remark on the resemblance between the duty placed and what they thought was I.C.I.'s profit margin.

It was a nice, comfortable world, and there was little sense of urgency evident anywhere. Thus I.C.I. had grown fat, and it was fat that could be trimmed if anyone bothered – as they have since demonstrated ('since' being after Mr Chambers' vertical integration ideas took a beating).

But it must be said in Mr Chambers' defence that he inherited a company used to having its way and unused to competition. Its bureaucracy was extensive, slow, and sluggish for there was little opposition on the home market which could not be steamrollered. This was no incentive to efficiency. Competition could not, however, be pushed around right across the board for in some fields I.C.I. was the small man. The I.C.I. Paints Division is a good example of one branch of activity where I.C.I. eventually began to run something like a commercial set-up. The picture in other fields was not so bright. The nylon producer, British Nylon Spinners (jointly owned with Courtaulds, with I.C.I. providing the polymer) boomed as there was an ever-increasing demand for nylon. Even so by the end of the fifties nylon still only took up about ten to twelve per cent of British synthetic fibre production. (One could indeed wish that the clothes manufacturers had kept up with B.N.S. To this day I wear shirts made from B.N.S. yarn; but the only satisfactory ones I have ever had were made in Sweden, from exported B.N.S. yarn.)

And here we come to the Courtaulds affair, in which the I.C.I. public relations department discovered among other things that I.C.I. are not a branch of government and that the General Motors rule did not in their case apply. This affair gives away more clues about the basic I.C.I. philosophy – and incidentally does more to reveal the mess they had got themselves into – than any other event in recent I.C.I. history. Part of the trouble stemmed from I.C.I.'s own ventures into synthetic fibres: Terylene (where in 1955 they were still talking of 'this new synthetic', though they had had the Terylene licence eight years), and Orlon. The first eventually went into production; as for the second, they obtained the licence from Du Pont, and then decided not to go into production. The problems in both cases were largely due to I.C.I.'s lack of experience in the production of textiles. Dithering apart, the position of I.C.I. as a basic producer was a difficult one. That I.C.I. (in *This is Our Concern*, 1955) produced and marketed some 12,000 different products from approximately 100 factories strung out over the length and breadth of Britain, and that only a handful of I.C.I. products could be bought over a counter, was seen as something to be proud of. 'They are', said I.C.I., at its most pompous, to round off the introduction, 'the vital raw materials on which the great manufacturing industries of Britain depend.'

And once again, yes but . . . That this number of products and plants was the best method of ensuring that I.C.I. continued unrationalized evidently struck no one inside the firm – or if it did there was certainly no evidence forthcoming from I.C.I. With these attitudes went a cumbersome decentralized organization (which in effect created a lot of private empires) and the knowledge that I.C.I. was safe behind their cardboard tariff barriers on which the sun, it seemed, would never set. If I.C.I. was a high-cost producer, with a corresponding lack of cost consciousness, if it picked the wrong processes, or if plants took a long time to construct, who needed to worry? The most famous example of wrong plant picking was the acrylonitrile plant at Billingham, capital cost £3$\frac{1}{2}$ million. It stood unproductive almost from the time of completion. I.C.I. discovered too late that newer processes meant that acrylonitrile could be produced much cheaper elsewhere. Indeed, in the end they even had to import it from the United States to fulfil their own contracts. The reason? Purely cost. They just could not get anywhere near world market prices. The reaction was understandable. At the start of the sixties, I.C.I. suddenly found itself faced with the prospect of the Common Market, with the possibility that it might for the first time have to cope with serious home competition, and that the carving up of markets or cartel arrangements was no longer as practicable as it had been in the twenties and thirties. It would be pleasant to conjure up an Ealing picture of panic in the boardrooms; but I cannot say whether this was so. Certainly to the outside observer it looked like it. The first result was a hasty, ill-thought-out announcement, the essence of which was that I.C.I. had discovered Europe, and that they were going to install plant there – to do, it seemed, what everyone else was already doing. (It has since changed considerably. Now they talk of their £100 million Rotterdam venture as eventually to 'manufacture products that don't yet exist, invented by people who are not yet working for us'.)

This was one approach to a solution. There were others. They began to overhaul the near feudal organization and eventually in 1962 called in management consultants to advise them. They began to think more in terms of commercial exports outside preference areas – though of course almost as immediately took to trade with the Soviet block, for like much of the rest of British industry I.C.I. has a penchant for dealing with governments. This was not so much due to delusions of grandeur as seemingly a sense of the fitting, the correct order of things; that if gentlemen must soil their hands with trade, dealing with governments is respectable – not to say easier.

One cannot, however, plan a company's future on so tenuous a basis. What worried I.C.I. was that they were very exposed to competition if the tariff barriers went down. With so few consumer products there were not many guaranteed outlets for most of their output; the problem was to obtain them. In free market conditions, high cost structure I.C.I. was not really essential to all its commercial customers, though the government might well see to it that some defence requirements would mean parts of I.C.I. remaining in business. And so began the long process of acquiring tied outlets, of which the Courtauld affair was a by-product. More successfully they expanded into wallpaper to give themselves a sure outlet for some of their paints, they tied Fisons for a further twenty years to an I.C.I. ammonia supply, and they expanded activity in similar ways in many other fields. At the same time they began the long process of staff rationalization which has since cut their numbers down from over 110,000 to 93,000.

The I.C.I. awakening to the outside world was an interesting one. It saw the beginnings of a sales drive outside the barriers of Commonwealth preference. In the three years 1958–60 while Commonwealth sales grew by nearly £3 million to just over £36 million, sales outside the Commonwealth grew by nearly £23 million to near the £100 million mark. But much of these sales have had only a temporary cushioning effect, for the fields in which I.C.I. is commercially a master are not always the most complex; and these are the areas of business activity in which everyone else is strong, usually also first on the chemical production list for any country setting out on the road to industrialization and planning a chemical capacity. As *European Chemical News* put it in early 1962, 'Viewed quite objectively in the light of present marketing conditions, international giants of I.C.I.'s stature are seen to be vulnerable to world forces to a much higher degree than are smaller concerns.' This is true also of the real giants of the industry, the large capacity plants of America, and the rapidly growing planned large capacity plants of France, Germany, and Italy – particularly the last – yet it has not stopped them from plant and other expansion.

Here we leave I.C.I., except to consider it in the context of the chemical industry generally. The chemical industry is the most international of businesses in that few people keep secrets to themselves: they either let them out on licence to foreign manufacturers, or make use of them by putting up plants abroad. These are the company-controlled products, for which there is usually a substitute, so that there are few real product monopolies – though those there are usually come in key areas. In the more basic materials, the techniques are almost universal: in many products, almost all you need to set yourself up in business is the capital. There is, however, no guarantee that you will be able to stay in business by following this practice. The only way in which a near guarantee can be found is by investing heavily in research and development, and then following it up with economic production.

There has been considerable argument about how much should be spent on research. Among the large European companies five per cent of annual turnover is not unusual, with product development taking another one or two per cent, sometimes more. The British average for both is much lower – less than three per cent. Even then one cannot be sure that all, most, or even a little of the work done will be productive. The complexities of much of modern chemical research are such that while the lone versatile, gifted, or just plain lucky amateur may stand a chance in some other industrial fields, his chances of making a discovery here are almost nil. Research in this industry demands sizeable teams, laboratories, expensive equipment, and possibly pilot plant. Most of the simple permutations have been worked to death. Now the industry's requirements are such that they call for complex substances. This means not only concentration of research facilities, but also that one should be most chary of talking in percentage terms when comparing research expenditure. It is of little use saying that we spend here as many per cent as the industry of Country x on research, when its industry is four or five times the size of ours. The chances of a comparable advance on a front just as wide are much smaller. This is true both in national and company terms. (Mr Chambers spotted this some time ago, and is now doing something about it. I.C.I.'s research is being concentrated.) Advances made are not only smaller, but there is a further compound effect. Too wide a dispersal of resources will mean that much of the research will have insufficient money, men, or equipment to play with. A project that might have taken three years will take five. Though success may result, there is almost no percentage in research which produces results even as little as five minutes after someone else has applied for a patent or produced an equivalent (unless your costs are much cheaper or you can rely on extensive tariff protection). A lot of firms have burned their fingers this way.

Presuming, however, that research is successful, the company is then faced with problems of production. It is here that the innate conservativeness of much of our industry begins to show up. Installed capacities are low, geared usually to a firm's own requirements (much of the industry's production is in intermediates for its own use) and those of its own home market. It is an old axiom (common not only to chemicals and to which I shall return again and again) that the larger the plant and the more intensively it is worked, the cheaper the product. This is not, of course, a never-ending cost reduction. In all plant-capacity planning, you eventually arrive at a point where costs level out. (In that most basic of chemicals, sulphuric acid, for example, this is between 180,000 and 250,000 tons capacity, depending on the process and the country – for plant costs differ. Almost needless to say, most of our plants are smaller.) And from there on, costs per ton produced are the same. When an industry such as this is so widespread, what happens is simple. Capacities are planned with other than economic cost factors in mind, plants are therefore usually smaller than the lowest cost capacity plant, thereby putting up the unit cost. This still does not complete the cycle. Even if chemicals are exported (effectively, dumped) at the prevailing world price, the squeeze on the profit margin will be greater than that on the same product from a plant of the right economic capacity. This in its turn has the further effect of generally reducing earnings, and so hindering further growth and investment. The way out for a small country is simple. Its manufacturers must be prepared to take a bigger risk than their competitors in countries with larger markets. And this depends in turn on an industry's belief in its selling ability which generally has to be further based on the belief of its members that they have the right product not only at the right price, but also at one that is economically sound.

And so the wheel turns full circle, for the industry gives few signs that it has had this confidence. America apart, is there anyone else who has? Again one turns to Europe. The report of a British Chemical Industry Productivity Survey of Germany and Italy published in 1963 found that from 1950 investment per employee in Italy was over £640 annually, £430 in West Germany, and nearly £320 in the United Kingdom. Germany, with an industry comparable in size to the British, yet exported 40 per cent more. Italy and Germany are both distinguished by the fact that like us they have to export to survive. They have not had the benefits of tied markets, though in many areas the German task was largely to re-create ties which existed before the war. The Italians have found an outlet in the Soviet block. They have differed too in goods sold, with the Germans once again selling complex dyes and pharmaceuticals the world over, and the Italians heavily involved in the sale of basic chemicals to the Eastern block and the underdeveloped countries – something which large-scale planning and lower Italian costs make possible.

The prime reason for the better performance put up by the Continentals is a lack of aversion to innovation (which is one of our basic problems here, and will also recur time and again throughout this book). Thus while our chemical industry was involved in the so-called plastics revolution right from the start, the attitudes seemed mainly to be concerned with plastics as substitutes, not materials in their own right. The unwillingness to recognize that new materials sometimes need new methods if they are to be produced economically is the main reason why we are backward in the new synthetic rubbers, and why when the oil pipeline revolution exists on the ground in Continental Europe here it is as yet only on paper. The Continental willingness to adapt to modern conditions has produced a higher rate of growth; since 1950 this has averaged 15 per cent a year in Italy, over 12 per cent in Germany – here it has been less than 6 per cent. In the case of the Continentals, growth has not only been a cause, but also an effect.

We have been hampered, as has been pointed out, by small plants. The smallness of the plant is indeed often the reason why a manufacturer, having geared his production to a home market, has to give long delivery dates to overseas customers, who immediately alternative sources of supply are available will go elsewhere. The smallness of plant has yet another effect: it means that few companies really know what their plant can do. Unlike some of the larger internationals they cannot after all afford to construct it themselves. This leads to the segregation of much of the industry into narrow fields of activity. And here the effects of too narrow educational specialization make themselves felt. Not only do many companies not know their plant, they also do not realize how much most of the chemical industry has in common. How can they? A company is only as good as its manpower. And so we get specializations where none really exist. Many of these are just as comprehensible to plant engineers also concerned with the mechanics of fluid flow in industries commonly thought to bear little relation to chemicals.

Is there then any field of activity in which one can say the British chemical industry has a good post-war record? Not surprisingly – for the record could not be all bad – there is one field of specialization in which the industry has done very well. This is the pharmaceuticals sector, or as it prefers to be called, the pharmaceuticals 'industry'. But to all intents and purposes the British pharmaceuticals industry does not exist. At least two-thirds of the industry (some people put it higher, at three-quarters) is owned by foreigners, mainly Americans and Swiss. Most of them have appeared here in the post-war years, for the National Health Service was to prove a godsend. Perhaps as important, however, has been the American weighing-up of British managerial talent and activity that this invasion has implied. These firms did not start off with much of the market, but they have built their share up. And though the Americans operated at the start largely with products developed by their home companies, what has proved interesting has been to watch some of their British laboratories begin to turn out products also at a high rate.

This broad picture then gives some idea of the problems which confront our chemical industry. Of all the major growth industries the chemical one is the least subject to government control and direction. (It often calls for assistance, which it almost invariably gets, but this is a different thing.) Yet during the fifties it has almost stood by and watched while one of its most prosperous markets – pharmaceuticals – has largely been taken over by other people.

It has missed opportunities. Ignoring economics and preferring to shelter quietly behind its almost absolute tariff barrier protection have been led to high costs, and a slowness to innovate. This in its turn has led to an isolation of much of the industry on the international scene, for the larger international groupings (particularly in complex petrochemicals where in realistic commercial installation we have usually been anything from five years behind, though we have had the knowhow) have preferred to put their serious investments elsewhere.

Nor have the industry's managements generally taken advantage of the export opportunities open to them, even in those products we do make, or taken more than a passing, almost academic, interest in the creation of the larger markets of the industrialized world, until the cream has been taken off by other countries. This again in spite of the fact in many fields the industry has had both the technical expertise and the products.

No one, I hope, will expect that a real industry will at all times and in all parts conform absolutely to any pure economic model. One can expect that some parts will, even if they should do so by no more than chance or accident. Perhaps then the major charge that needs to be made is this: in anything resembling working model terms, the British chemical industry – as the evidence will, I think, have shown – still does not exist. This is at the heart of the industry's difficulties, and this is the responsibility of its management, a responsibility to which they seem to have awoken only recently.

Chapter 4

Guided Weapons: Failure through Lateness

This chapter and the two which follow it deal with sectors of industry closely linked by defence, for which automatically the government is the largest customer. They are missiles, aircraft, and electronics – three industrial sectors often indissolubly linked. In the case of the first two groups of products, however, the government – whether through the services or the nationalized airlines – is the main customer in a far different sense from the normal industrial purchaser, however large. The government theoretically has these weapons and aircraft built for it by private industry. In practice private industry seldom has much room for manoeuvre. The government pays for much of its research, awards contracts almost on 'buggin's turn' principles – we shall meet this again – effectively controls profit margins and export prices, and generally seems to operate on the principle that if there is a loss to be made private industry should make it but a profit is something to be shared. All this has had considerable effects on the development of these industries, which at times cease to bear much relation to commercial organizations at all. Any detailing of the recent history of these industries should tell us something about the way in which they are managed; should tell us, too, something of the way in which government deals with an industry when it is the main or sole customer. Above all, it should also tell us something about management within government, the ability of the machine at the politician's command to cope with the technological world we live in, and its standards of skill and probity.

Whether or not this country should have nuclear weapons and their carriers is a question about which almost anyone when prodded will turn out to have strong feelings – even if they have previously given it little thought. It is not an argument in which I intend to join here. What does concern me are the economic and industrial implications of any weapons programme, whether for crossbows or V-bomber, anti-aircraft guided weapons or missiles with nuclear warheads. These notes then are the bare bones of the guided weapons story since the war, and the conclusions we can draw from it. The story itself too poses the question: did anyone ever expect that these weapons – as produced – could ever do what was to be expected of them? This is a vital question for as defence is possibly the last subject which can be discussed in a vacuum, the answer should tell us whether the money could have been spent to better purpose.

At the outset we can say five things about the overall guided weapons programme. First, it has provided much of the little dynamic that has been at all evident in British industry. Second, it has also provided the best example we have of the failure of the governmental machinery to cope with the technological society. Third, it has been surrounded by more humbug and nonsense than almost any other area of our industrial life. Fourth, since the end of the war there is no record of any new guided weapon having been delivered on schedule. Fifth and last, there is no record either of any government-sponsored weapon having been provided at a cost within that of the original estimates by a factor of three.

The story of missile and guided weapons development is perhaps the most important part of any examination of the defence industries. Not only has it taken up a large share of government spending on defence orders, but it also gives some indication of how unequipped we are as a society to cope with, keep a check on, and keep up with the newer branches of technology.

We begin with the smallest weapons. Since the First World War, infantrymen have had two overriding operational problems to contend with: how to cope on the one hand with tanks and armoured carriers, and on the other with aircraft. Of the last the most important has become the low-flying strike aircraft. Given a satisfactory weapon against both, or even a chance against them, the infantryman in action will be as happy as he is ever likely to be. Though a lot of research has been devoted to this problem, foolproof solutions are not possible – we just do the best we can. This is the first group of weapons and projects we need to consider, and they are few.

The second group of weapons is again mainly defensive: those concerned with anti-aircraft defence not only of individual men but also of installations. These include aircraft- and ship-carried anti-aircraft missiles, as well as the land-based batteries of weapons which have replaced the conventional anti-aircraft guns of the last war.

The third group consists of offensive weapons for tactical purposes. Into this comes the tactical atomic artillery with which the British Army of the Rhine is equipped, the surface-to-surface short-range missiles, and the aircraft-carried strike weapons, all of which can carry a nuclear warhead.

The fourth and last group is the one which normally causes all the fuss (at the same time obscuring what is going on elsewhere). These are the strategic nuclear weapon carriers, the ballistic missiles of all ranges, the aircraft-carried stand-off weapons and the Polaris-type missiles in their submarines – or elsewhere.

Currently we operate weapons in all these classes, with two exceptions, inter-continental range ballistic missiles and infantry weapons for dealing with low-flying aircraft. In the field of strategic missiles, we have the medium range obsolescent Thors (these were American built, as are the army's atomic artillery, and the surface-to-surface tactical atomic weapons, Honest John and Corporal). Except for a couple of portable weapons which we buy from Australia and Sweden and which are not in the nuclear carrier class, we build the rest ourselves. They are manufactured by a group of main contractors: the British Aircraft Corporation in the form of English Electric, Bristol, and Vickers; Rolls Royce, G.E.C., Ferranti, and Shorts, and Hawker Siddeley in the form of De Havillands, closely supported by a number of smaller firms and subsidiaries, many of them involved in electronics. The weapons they are manufacturing or have under development can be grouped into the classes we have indicated quite closely. For the infantry, we have the Vigilant and the Malkara – an Australian development – both by current standards easily portable, cheap, and accurate weapons, useful though not 100 per cent certain against just about anything except aircraft. For aircraft field defence, however, the infantryman still has to depend on developments of the unsatisfactory weapons which armed his predecessors in the Second World War, for no one has as yet come up with anything sufficiently effective, though a requirement has existed for years.

What's Wrong with British Industry?

When we turn to the second group, we find that (irrespective of the public argument about strategy) in practice this has represented the overriding preoccupation of the Ministry of Defence. It is in this field that the majority of failures and successes have been scored, and here also that the bulk of the money has been spent. Here we have the land-based guided weapons which take up where the anti-aircraft guns of the last war left off. These are the Bristol Ferranti Bloodhound, one of the few successes of the guided weapons programme, and the English Electric Thunderbird, one of its major failures. On the aircraft-carried side we have the Firestreak and Red Top; and for the ship and naval aircraft weapons we have the Short Sea Cat and Hawker Siddeley Sea Slug.

As far as British industry is concerned, the third class of weapons is non-existent for here we are dependent on America. The last British project was for the short-range surface-to-surface nuclear-weapon carrier Blue Water, which was cancelled in August 1962. Otherwise we rely on Honest John, the army's American-built atomic artillery, and the American air-to-ground weapon Bull Pup. When we turn to the nuclear-weapon carriers proper, we have first the free-fall bombs carried by the V-bomber Force; second, Blue Steel, originally developed as a short-range stand-off weapon; third, the Thor missiles, which are now being scrapped. Fourth we are developing a new longer range version of Blue Steel to replace the cancelled American Skybolt; this is to be in service within the next three years. Fifth we will eventually have Polaris (if of course the government has not changed its mind by the time it is built and becomes operational).

This is a very quick tour of the current scene, and at first glance one would think this an impressive list. When government money is involved, however, life is never quite as simple as that. To understand what has been happening in the guided weapons field one needs to go back to its origins: back to the last years of the war. Two things got us into the business, one the appearance of German missiles, the other the problem of the Kamikazes, the Japanese suicide planes. These problems were given to a small army team to solve, but by the time they were properly started the war was over. It is from the work of this team that we obtained the first official British guided weapon, a beam rider powered by a scaled down German v-2 motor. It was called RTV One (Rocket Test Vehicle One) and was to be finally proved in 1954 when it shot down a Firefly target aircraft. As its name implies, it was a test vehicle, and from its development stems Sea Slug. That there was a six-year interregnum is not to be blamed on the team which built it, for the muddle and the indecision had already started, as had the Services empire building. The causes were largely cutbacks in expenditure, the lack of a rearmament programme, and perhaps more important the generally indecisive atmosphere.

The Labour government, in this case advised by Sir Ben Lockspeiser, decided that all missile research should come under the Royal Aircraft Establishment's Farnborough umbrella. Farnborough's knowledge of guided weapons development at this time was practically nonexistent. (Most of the early work had been done at the Rocket Projectile Establishment at Westcott.) At the same time Lockspeiser managed to kill the supersonic aircraft project, and both decisions were to cost us dear. They involved a great many people in one of these administrative shake-ups which, while they look nice and dramatic on paper, do a lot to waste the time of the few people who do know what they are doing. One of the old-timers in the guided weapons business maintains that this shake-up cost us two years' development time – something we obviously could not afford. Meanwhile, another private empire was after a fashion flourishing. This was the one based on Anti-Aircraft Command and General Pyle which (in cooperation with the R.A.F.) produced an abortive missile leading to a test vehicle, in this case known as CTV One, or Components Test Vehicle One. This progressed through a project for an air-to-air weapon called Blue Sky (believed to have cost over £15 million), and eventually became Fireflash.

It is unwise to progress too fast, for by doing so one ignores the crucial time for guided weapons development, the late 1940s and the first two years of the fifties. It is at this period that the majority of the specifications for the weapons now in service were laid down. Thus we find that the specification for what is now Sea Slug, one of the weapons currently in use, was decided in 1949. The original cost estimates for the development of this sea-to-air weapon were under £2 million, the actual cost rising over the years to around £40 million. The first recorded successful firing of Sea Slug, armed with warhead and fuse, took place in 1957. Thus some eight years had elapsed between the parent test weapon and a suitable-for-production direct descendant. Though it is not strictly part of this story, in fact Sea Slug was ready a considerable time before either its launchers or its ships. This not only helped to retard its development; it meant that by the time it was ready, the 'enemy' aircraft it was designed to cope with were no longer in service. (This has also happened to other weapons.) It meant too that no sooner was it in production than the Ministry had to consider beginning the development of its successor, Sea Slug Two, which is scheduled to cost even more. It was built by Armstrong Whitworth Aviation, Sperrey and G.E.C. These firms are also responsible for Sea Slug Two.

Meanwhile, the continued existence of air forces and manned bomber threats as well as the continuous government acceptance of the Royal Air Force's fighter defence role had seen to it that there was a demand for air-to-air weapons. The CTV One venture had resulted in Fireflash, and a series of homing weapons, the first of which was Firestreak from De Havilland. These were not the only projects in the pipeline, for Ministerial coordination was almost non-existent, and civil-service and armed-forces rivalries abounded. So we got odd projects appearing out of the blue, whose existence was almost unknown to the official coordinators (some of whom, just to improve the situation, were also busy dreaming up projects of their own). There is a fabulous weapon from this time (the early fifties) called Blue Boar. Originally meant to be used against battleships, this came from a test vehicle by R.A.E. and Vickers, which was taken over as an official project. It was for an aircraft-carried flying bomb fitted with a television camera in its nose. It was guided to the target by the pilot who saw in effect what the bomb saw on a monitor screen in the aircraft. The television techniques of the early fifties, however, were such that television cameras required considerable light to operate by, so that at night the bomb was blind! This project was cancelled when nuclear warheads became available and is thought to have cost the country over £8 million.

The next on the list was an Air-Ministry-backed surface-to-surface missile of 400 miles' range called Red Rapier. It would be better to call this a pilotless aircraft fitted with a warhead. Its development was advanced, the snags were beginning to show, and the cost had mounted to some £5 million when it was cancelled. The cancellation was due both to assurances of bigger and better projects in the pipeline and to the need to find someone who could manufacture a better air-to-air weapon for the country's defence equipment manufacturing facilities which were then under strain. The need for this 'better' weapon had been foreseen as far back as 1951 when it became obvious that the succession of projects which produced Firestreak, and Red Top, all had one disadvantage: they were heat homers with considerable operational disadvantages. The result was the Red Dean project, to be built by Vickers, Smiths, E.M.I., and G.E.C. This was a crash programme for a complex air-to-air weapon to end all weapons. It was to be carried by the Gloster Javelin, an aircraft which too had run into development difficulties. Many millions of pounds had been spent when in 1956 the programme was cancelled, almost without warning: not long after, the government cancelled the Javelin.

Meanwhile, back at the ranch, developments of some of the original weapons were still continuing. In 1955, Fireflash started hitting targets. By that time, however, the Fireflash had been seen as the right weapon to arm an emergency aircraft, the Supermarine Swift. It was an emergency aircraft for a simple reason: at the start of the Korean operations the Air Force had found itself without a swept-wing fighter of Mig class. This had resulted in another crash programme to produce two aircraft, the Swift and the Hunter. The Swift was not successful, and was cancelled. With it went the chance of an operational version for Fireflash. The Ministry kindly enough said to Fairey's 'We will use it as a training weapon, but better weapons of this class are on the way.' The first result of this was that Fairey's were unable to sell the weapon abroad, and one successful missile nearly as promptly went out of production. The successful weapon on the way was the De Havilland Firestreak, the infra-red homer whose successor is Red Top (see above). This too dated from the days of 1948–9 when most of the preliminary specifications were laid down. De Havilland's had been working on it since 1950 – publicly admitting to 1951 – but no sooner was Fairey's Fireflash effectively scrapped than it was found that we were having trouble with Firestreak. The cause of the trouble was the usual one; the weapon was proved for operations up to 15,000 feet; the operational requirements were for a weapon to operate at 45,000 feet.

Meanwhile at one of the other ranches work was in hand on two surface-to-air weapons, the English Electric Thunderbird (cost

£53 million) and the Bristol Ferranti Bloodhound (cost £50 million). These had arisen from an original requirement in 1949 for a surface-to-air guided weapon to replace anti-aircraft guns. No one in those days (apart from Dr Barnes Wallis) seemed to know what ramjets or moving wings could do. Accordingly the job given to English Electric was for a rocket-propelled fixed-wing anti-aircraft weapon. The Bristol Ferranti combination meanwhile were working on the same task, but using moving targets and ramjets, and were to test-fire the Bloodhound successfully in 1957, a year before Thunderbird. In the process they very nearly put paid to English Electric's G.W. activities, for the results of both tests showed that while the Bloodhound had the high altitude (up to 65,000 feet) but was limited in ground range by the guidance systems (something remediable) the Thunderbird was limited in its range by its propulsion system. The commercial result was striking, the Army were given Thunderbird and there were no further sales, while Bristol Ferranti sold the Bloodhound not only to the Royal Air Force, but also to Sweden, Switzerland, and Australia.

We cannot as yet leave this story, for we have not even now mentioned all the major products of the industry. We still have to deal with Blue Steel, Blue Streak, and Blue Water (the colour in front of the names is now in fact meaningless. Originally it indicated the class of weapons, then someone realized that it gave the game away during development), Orange William, Green Ranger, Swingfire, and Bloodhound. First, Orange William, a project for another complex dual-purpose anti-tank/anti-aircraft weapon. This was another of those 'too classy to work' projects (as one of its industrial critics called it in 1957) – and it was finally cancelled in 1959. Swingfire, an on-again, off-again weapon, now in production, is of the same general specification. This too stems from development work of Fairey's.

A single-purpose low-level anti-aircraft missile to which little attention has been paid was PT428, or Green Ranger. This too did not come off. Original cost estimates were under £3 million; final cost was thought to be between £10 and £15 million, some of which was spent with English Electric before it was cancelled.

The Blue Streak story is of course well known. This liquid-fuelled missile by De Havilland was obsolescent before it was even started and – a result of the crash programme – was built under conditions which would not be considered good by any production engineer, and could only be fairly described as a mess. Scheduled to cost £50 million it was eventually officially admitted to have cost £107 million, at which cost it had never got beyond tethered firings. The calculations made showed that to carry on its development and production would have cost nearly £500 million more, for the estimates to continue the programme and bring it into service by 1963 were of the order of £6000 million. Nor do the official cost figures necessarily represent the truth. Many of these are believed to be underestimates, the opportunities for concealment are many, and they are often used. There is, for example, considerable suspicion that expenditure on Blue Streak was above the figure given, some people putting it as high as £140 million all told. All the costs I give are minimum figures.

Blue Water, the solid-fuelled equivalent to the American Sergeant, was built by English Electric. The programme started in 1956 called for a 50-mile-range Army-operated land-based missile with a nuclear warhead. By the time the operation was cancelled in 1962 this had cost us £25 million – after progress which made the engineers responsible almost spit blood.

Blue Steel, an Avro development from 1953, is the stand-off weapon which should arm our V-bomber force. This has cost so far over £100 million (some people say as much as £150 million) and again progress is not good. Bloodhound III: this was a project that never came off. We have not so far discussed Blue Steel's successor – a hurried mock-up which may or may not eventually replace the Skybolts we did not get – the problems of a British Polaris, Swingfire, CF299, a project for a small ship anti-aircraft weapon, or whether we should have Sea Slug II for another £70 million; and I do not intend to do so.

These are some of the weapons of the future (there are others) and should stay wrapped in security – though the position of the last few years does not give one confidence that the security will exist, that they will be ready on time, do the job they are meant to, or even bear any cost relation to the estimates (whatever these may have been). These programmes for scrapped weapons have all told so far cost more than £600 million on these unofficial estimates and more than £800 million according to some inspired guesses. (I have heard one putting it at £1,000 million.)

Spread over the years, this is not very large.

What's Wrong with British Industry?

In terms of overall resources, however, it has tied up many of the skills which could have been better used elsewhere, for what do we have as a result? Of the missiles named, only Firestreak, Sea Slug, Red Top, Sea Cat, Thunderbird, Bloodhound, and Blue Steel have ever seen service. Of these the first is obsolete, and all the rest obsolescent. There is in fact only one guided weapon in service which has ever come up on time within the original estimates. This is the anti-tank weapon Vigilant, and it is noticeable that this weapon was a private venture whose development was paid for by Vickers.

This gives one clue to what has been going on. The crash programme of the early fifties resulted in wartime approval of cost-plus, and it was not until the cancellations caused by the 1957 Defence White Paper and its 'we are going nuclear' emphasis that it was realized how much we had been spending. Of course, the cut back was a gradual process, leaving many firms in the industry either hurt, and correspondingly not keen to take on further work, or still too busy to do so. Though estimates have been called for, they have been of the sort which state: 'We have x pounds to spend, whoever comes nearest to it will get the contract.'

And here there is a further complication. Though, in very general terms, the guided weapons programme has been overseen by R.A.E., at no time has there been a continuous basic research programme. The major research has been tied to contracts for particular weapons. The result is that when a weapon is cancelled, research on that set of problems ceases. This does not, as might appear, make sense, for the guided weapons programme has many common problems to cope with. What happens is that the next contractor in the field has to try to carry on where the other one left off, without usually having the same basic information or a design team as up to date with the latest knowhow. (This last in practice led to inter-company raiding for personnel.) Result? Another weapon likely to come late into service.

In the missile business as in many others, Treasury cheese-paring, say some industrialists, is likely to have cost tens if not hundreds of millions. This in its turn has another effect. The ever-rising costs of missile developments have been partly due to the overloading of work forces – in attempts to catch up with un-realistic time schedules. The guided weapons business being an offshoot of the aircraft industry, it has been fitted into normal aircraft-industry company structures. And as the real experts have had to be placed at the top, this has meant time and again that the few – and they are pitifully few – experts have been so bogged down in administration that they hardly ever saw the project they were supposed to be involved with. And the scramble to obtain missile design teams was due not only to their knowhow, but also the lack of suitably qualified recruits available to take their place. Engineers equipped to work in this field are at a premium, and even more precious than the scientists whose lack is being constantly bemoaned. Staff must be found from somewhere, so the industry has made do with scientists who also could have been better used elsewhere.

Perhaps the main causes of worry, however, have been the three following. First, the business has been largely in the hands of the aircraft industry at a time when it was still run by prima donnas more interested in prestigious flying machines, so that it has not been run as efficiently as would have been the case had the business been handled by more commercially conscious industries. Second, like all defence industry, it suffers from an occupational hazard which can be simply described as wasting time talking to, with, and at the government and its administrative machine – which some executives maintain takes one day in five. Last, government apart, not all of the programme is under the industry's own direct control. For every worker directly involved, there are at least two in support activities elsewhere, usually in electronics, or in the associated aircraft engine companies. (Involvement has spread further than this; such companies as I.C.I. have been involved in the chemical fuels and engineering; and the engineering demands made because of miniaturization, high temperatures, and many other stresses to which these weapons are subject have spread the work load across companies in such fields as glass, synthetic fibres, non-ferrous metals, general engineering, and the machine tools and capital plant industries.)

Before we leave missile development, two final observations must be made. We are likely to be faced with further redundancy problems in the industry during this and the coming years as the Thunderbird, Bloodhound, and Blue Steel programmes are run down. A near 40,000 skilled labour force depending directly and indirectly on this work may well be cut in half during the same period (though one doubts if they have been warned). Indeed the process has already begun.

The second observation takes us back to one major premise, the general unpreparedness of the government machine in its dealings with the technological age. This story shows that government cost estimating has proved wildly innaccurate and the industry has been asked to do things at prices which bear little or no relation to actuality. The error has then been compounded by the Government taking the easy way out in times of economic stringency. The almost annual cuts in defence spending have usually been cuts in purchasing and development, thus spreading the programme out over a longer period. (The constant rise in salaries and wages, though the total paper defence bill has remained constant, has meant too a further cut in the money available for re-equipment – which seems to get smaller every year, though the rate of change in weapons seems to be increasing.) Development difficulties apart (and these can always be expected), is it any wonder that by the time weapons appear they are often out of date? If, that is, their lateness has not already led to cancellation.

Chapter 5

Aircraft: The Failure of Government

The aircraft industry is really three closely tied and intermingled industrial sectors, the aircraft designers and builders themselves or 'airframe' manufacturers, the engine manufacturers, and the electronics and instrumentation companies. (We have already met many of these companies in Chapter 4.) Since the government-inspired amalgamations of 1959, the first group consists of three major and three smaller companies, respectively Hawker Siddeley (which incorporated A.V. Roe, Armstrong Whitworth, Gloster, Hawker, De Havilland and Folland, in a tight group organization with considerable central direction), the British Aircraft Corporation (Vickers Armstrong Aircraft, English Electric Aviation, Bristol, Hunting, in a much looser form of organization with the companies retaining considerable independence), and Westland Aircraft, manufacturers of helicopters (Westlands, Fairey Aviation, Saunders Roe, and the helicopter side of Bristols). The three smaller companies are Handley Page, Short Brothers and Harland, and British Executive and General Aviation, the last a Pressed Steel subsidiary manufacturing light aircraft. There are two main engine firms, Bristol Siddeley, half owned by Hawker and half by Bristol, and Rolls Royce, which has supplied over half the engines for turbine-powered aircraft now flying. Lastly, the industry is closely supported by instrument and electronics manu-facturers: Smiths, Dowty, Elliotts, E.M.I., Pye, Decca, Marconi, and almost every other major company with electrical and elec-tronic interests in the country.

This is the industry – what does it do? The industry's final production over the last few years has averaged about £400 million a year, with exports since 1956 fluctuating over the £100 million mark (though this may not in fact represent the real cost of the aircraft, for the government research and development contribution may – or may not – be included, according to the mood of the moment). They have in fact been as high as £156 million in 1959. This sum is a rough guide, for these overall figures do not indicate the changing pattern of manufacture and exports. Within the export total for example, while the sales value of civil aircraft has decreased, that of aero engines has risen. At the same time, the value of second-hand aircraft exported has also risen to a point where they have at times accounted for more than is raised by the sale of new aircraft. There is nothing wrong or reprehensible in this. The sales of new aircraft tend to fluctuate as new machines become available, for not every new machine in this world is competitive. The sales of second-hand aircraft, however, have shown a steady rise largely because prices have been low to the point where they were almost given away. It has been a case of either selling at give-away prices or not selling at all. As some of the complex financial arrangements between the aircraft manufacturers and the airlines depended on the repurchase of old aircraft by the manufacturers, as part of the price of sale of new ones, the manufacturers had little option but to capitalize on these as quickly as possible.

What, if anything, is wrong with the industry? For a start it has been so mucked about by the government that its leadership seems to have lost its nerve. Though acceptable customers are more numerous for aircraft than weapons, the industry has not commercially had anything like the same number of successes as it has had types of aircraft on offer. In fact the only post-war British civil aircraft so far sold which has shown anything resembling a reasonable profit has been the Viscount which, with sales of over 400,[1] became the second largest seller in the history of aviation (after the DC3, though it is worth pointing out that the DC3 got its boost into the thousands as a military aircraft during the Second World War). It has since been overtaken by the Boeing 707. The list of commercial flops, irrespective of cause, is a gloomy one. Hermes, Tudor, Ambassador, Britannia, Viking, Vanguard, Comet – all these have failed to make real headway on world markets. (The well-known Comet tragedy is of course a special case.) Apart from these there

1. It is unlikely that this would have been possible had it not been for a supply arrangement between Vickers and Rolls Royce which precluded the sale of Dart engines to anyone else till 1958.

have been the products which never, for one reason or another, went as far as series production, from the Bristol Brabazon and the Saro Princess flying-boats to the Fairey Rotodyne and the vc7, the civil version of the v1000.

What went wrong? To understand this it is necessary to understand also the industry's basic dependence on the government. It is now another cliché that we have for years been suffering from a great-industrial-power delusion. Yet this is one thing that we are not, at least in the sense that the United States and Russia are. We do not have the space, the population, or the sure markets and growth possibilities. The application of this to the aircraft industry should be simple and obvious, yet it is hard to think of a type of aircraft which we have not tried to make, and we usually try to make all of them at the same time. Again, we have been spreading our resources too thinly. This is something in which the industry has always acquiesced, and in the process has made its dependence on the government even more total. The industry now will no longer consider the production of civil aircraft without government support and British airline orders, and in both cases the taxpayer foots the bill. This, we know, was the price paid for the enforced amalgamations (the firms which refused to amalgamate have been left out in the cold. Both Shorts and Handley Page have had selling difficulties with the government ever since.)

That dependence, of course, begins elsewhere: with military aircraft. The post-war history of defence aviation is very similar to that of civil aircraft (indeed is the cause of much of the civil aircraft production problem), or that of guided weapons. It is one long story of cancelled projects. It has, however, had a more serious effect. So much money has been wasted that the public just cannot take it all in. Crash projects, with which the industry's history is littered, create work. But that is not all they do; they also create shortages of skilled manpower elsewhere. The skilled manpower pool is not inexhaustible, and the industry during the early 1950s raided almost everyone for skills. Even then there were never enough men to go round, so that progress was in any case not as fast as it should have been if time schedules were to be met.

The tale does not end here. The difficulty with crash programmes is that they become cost plus, and that a programme suddenly introduced may just as suddenly be withdrawn when the emergency is over. This can lead to wide fluctuations in company turnover, organization, production, and profits. When skilled labour is short companies tend to retain their work force. They cannot afford to let them go as the skills will be needed when the next orders come. That the orders will eventually come is almost certain, for defence is geared to other countries' capabilities – and we are generally too proud to buy in service aircraft. There will in any case be pressure from the companies for their orders. A cut-back can have a considerable effect on investors' confidence, as well as an effect on company morale and confidence. And of course there is the natural desire of companies to stay as large as they can, even though their growth was dictated not by the skill of management, but by considerations basically outside its control: the preoccupation of politicians with defence and foreign affairs.

The effects of this on an industry basically dependent on government spending have been considerable. Resources have not been concentrated on what would necessarily pay, but naturally enough on what the government wanted. (The Comet II, for example, should have been in series production and service long before it actually was. Leaving aside technical problems which caused some difficulties, the lateness was also due to the inability of De Havilland to do everything at once, for at the time they were also heavily involved in the Blue Streak programme.) The effect of the inability of the government to make up its mind and stick to it has also been felt on the civil aircraft side; programmes have been disrupted to enable the industry to cope with Service requirements.

The crash and other defence programmes have had another and perhaps more serious effect. The close links forged since the war have been such that too often the companies look like Service organizations in plain clothes. Now the Services are notoriously wasteful of manpower, and lack cost-consciousness. These traits have been carried over to the industry, whose lack of cost-consciousness is indeed a standing joke in the rest of British industry. Though the industry is plentifully provided with accountants, they are not cost accountants. Like other Service departments, their task seems mainly to be to account for every penny spent under one heading or another which will satisfy a Ministry, and not to see that the money was wisely spent. This is one of the reasons why aircraft company balance sheets really represent little more than audit figures and are not representative of what our fathers would have called commercial effort. The system runs under costing conditions which are almost totally unrealistic. How can it be otherwise when the companies are all the time operating under crisis conditions in which the accent is on production on whatever terms can be obtained and not on efficiency?

This is what happened during the fifties, and if there is any blame to be attached for such losses as say the £40 million lost on the Swift, or the near £150 million spent on the Victor bomber before it was discovered that it could not carry Skybolt, it must be shared on both sides. For 'both sides', however, one should really read three sides. The third lies in that complex of changing Ministries, Supply, Defence, Air, Aviation, and the Admiralty, which has been responsible for laying down the details of the programme, agreeing specifications, briefing ministers, and otherwise spending public money. The one inescapable conclusion that any examination of the State's aircraft research, development, and purchasing programmes reveals is the lack of technical competence among the civil servants and advisers which are – also inescapably – the machinery that governments have to use in their dealings with the industry. (Though the practice of lay Ministers cutting through this maze and dealing directly – in principle – is not unknown, this has usually resulted in just as bad a confusion.)

Lack of technical knowhow is not of course confined to Ministries dealing with the aircraft industry. It is found in many other government departments. The Treasury, the Board of Trade, the Ministry of Works, and the War Office, in fact almost any Ministry likely to come into contact with industry lacks specialist expertise. It is more damaging to the public purse, however, in the Ministries dealing with Service aviation simply because the sums involved are far larger than elsewhere, and the losses comparably greater.

There is, however, an allied problem which further complicates dealings between the State and the industry: this is the problem of State security (as distinct from commercial security), which can affect relations between Ministries and the industry in the civil aircraft sector. State security means that overworked civil servants – and their opposite numbers in the industry – find their area of competence limited. The practical effects of the security system we have – crudely over-simplified – is that there are hundreds of people milling about, each responsible for one minuscule area of activity, while the few people who can, and are allowed to, understand what is going on find themselves at tops of organization pyramids where their time is not taken up with the real work for which they are fitted, but with administration, organization, and non-productive paper work. It may be that the system has been designed to ensure that as few people as possible will know the full details of everything. In practice, the system allied to normal civil service routines results in almost endless self-defeating delays.

Naturally, the same problems do not apply in the same degree to the manufacture of civil aircraft, though even here problems do arise as much of the equipment owes its origins to Service requirements. One of the major problems, however, is caused by the structure of civil aviation, in which the government through its nationally owned airlines will have to foot the majority of the development and production bills. The relationship between Ministries, the manufacturers, and Services is different in tone from that of the relationship between Ministries, manufacturers, and airlines. The first contains a large element of strife and interdepartmental and inter-Service rivalry which has its effect on programmes. The second could almost be described as an incestuous triangle, in which the first party is a somewhat subservient member. The Ministries are tied by the requirements of the airlines and the inability of the aircraft industry to sell abroad in sufficient volume. Part of this last is caused by the industries' approach to overseas sales. There is a great delusion that something carrying the British hallmark of good skilled no-nonsense engineering is in fact enough. This is like the delusion that British capital products do not really need selling, that the Chairman only needs to whistle around the world with some pretty drawings and pictures in his briefcase, visiting his opposite numbers in foreign companies, saying effectively 'Here I am. You know me, I wouldn't waste your time or mine by coming out to sell you a dud product. What about it?' This is an exaggeration, but it does bear some resemblance to the general approach to sales (Westland aircraft, for example, the second largest helicopter manufacturer in Europe – we shall come to them in a minute – had nearly 130 named executives on the senior staff list in the 1961 annual report. Only one of these was a salesman!). Unfortunately, however, the product's technical excellence is not the only concern of operators. They wish to know that the product will be in service in time, and one of the deciding factors here is knowledge of the equipment that the opposition is flying. It is useless trying to sell a 500-mile-an-hour aircraft when the opposition is planning to put out an aircraft of the same capacity, and with the same break-even point load factor, which does 600 miles per hour. It is useless too offering aircraft suited to Commonwealth routes and stage lengths when what is wanted is something with another 500 miles range.

Government prevarication may make an aircraft turn out to be a dead loss, even though the machine itself may be a good one. Up at Belfast, Short Brothers are building the Belfast freighter. They will build ten, though the economic break-even point is thirty. Those ten will have cost us something like £4 million an aircraft, or £40 million all told by the time they are finished. The range of miscalculation here is great, for Short's should never have been allowed to start. To imagine that the Belfast, which has not yet flown, can sell in competition with the second-hand Britannias which are a drug on the market, or against say the competition of the Boeing 707 freighter, shows a considerable lack of commercial awareness somewhere. We know it was not at Short's, for the original plan envisaged that the government through its agencies would buy enough aircraft to get Short's at least to break-even point.

Another recent example of serious errors is to be found in the VC10. As I write, there is considerable doubt that the VC10 will be a commercial success. The troubles here are not solely concerned with technical teething problems – these have happened to aircraft manufacturers the world over, particularly when they are breaking new ground. The problem is simply one of specification. B.O.A.C., it seems, is not really able to forecast its requirements. (It is not of course alone. We have suffered a lot from imperial hangovers which made people plan as though the Empire still existed and depended on us to supply its communication links.) We need now not an aircraft fit to fly easy stages to Australia, but one capable of flying direct to the West Coast of America, something it seems for which the VC10 was not originally designed. And so, of course, the specifications change as the aircraft progresses, technical problems arise, and delays occur. Nothing, I think, indicates more clearly the servile – it is not too strong a word – attitude of Vickers to the government than the VC10 programme. This aircraft has all along been tailored to B.O.A.C. requirements, and they in turn asked for an aircraft to fly specific routes. That the result might well be a machine which would not fit anyone else's requirements, even though they would have to sell it elsewhere, does not seem to have crossed anyone's mind.

One should not single out Vickers for condemnation, for they are not alone in their sins. Until Beagle Aircraft began serious operations, the field of light civil aviation in this country was almost left to De Havilland's. Most of the aircraft produced were a by-product of military aviation, such as the communications aircraft, the Dove and the Chipmunk trainer. Light aircraft, however, are the ones not paid for by the public purse; they are, or should be, commercial propositions (though military sales are of course a help). But Beagle went into the business with no such surety, for we lack facilities for executive aircraft flying, and landing charges at Ministry of Aviation airfields are high. This was a field without competition, though at their time of entry the aircraft industry was in a sad state of disarray due to the recasting of the late fifties, and a light aircraft business would have been a useful asset and insurance in many companies.

Lastly, before considering the future of the industry, we must turn to Westlands, now Britain's helicopter industry. Possibly even more than the rest, Westlands is tied to official coat tails. The problems lie in the basic construction of the helicopters themselves. Power plants are only slowly becoming more efficient with the introduction of turbines. Fuel consumption is high, and the load factor is seldom as high as one third of all up weights, decreasing rapidly with longer range requirement. All in all, the large helicopter is not an economic proposition for civil operations, at least by today's standards – and all the helicopters operating scheduled services are subsidized. Needless to say we do not have any here, for in fact Westlands do not manufacture a helicopter of a size suitable for the most economic of passenger operations. For that we have to go to America. Neither have they as yet seriously bothered with light helicopters – also a promising commercial proposition. For those we again have to go to America, France, or Italy (though the last two will often be working with American patents!).

What Westlands do make are, again largely with American knowhow, military helicopters and their civilian counterparts for such people as B.U.A. (who have a charter fleet). This service concentration, and the security with which they are of course surrounded, means in theory a high-cost product difficult to sell on the open market. This is true in practice. Export sales where they exist are either to the Services of other Commonwealth countries such as Australia, or to our politically undesirable allies, such countries as Portugal and South Africa.

This then is a Cook's tour of the aircraft manufacturing industry. I have not so far dealt with the industry as a government research shop. The use of the word government here is necessary. We after all only have the rotatable engine and the VTOL aircraft, to pick but two, as a result of government requirements. (We might have been able to have Barnes Wallis's variable geometry Swallow Wing project nearer fruition by now if the government had not withdrawn support, and then decided to take it up again later when other countries showed interest in it.)

What, then, of the industry of the future? Is it fated to remain a handmaiden of the government? Certainly the current signs make it seem so. The majority of orders in the pipeline are defence orders, or orders for B.O.A.C. or B.E.A. The TSR2 – about which we shall no doubt hear a lot more – the Argosy, and the VTOL fighter for defence, the Trident, VC10, and the BAC111 for the rest, will keep the industry docile as ever. These and the Beagles, DH125s, H.P. Heralds, and the Avro748s do not – looking at the current order situation – exactly add up to a commercial volume of aircraft to keep a great industry going. And in the background there stands the monster that is Concord, which if past history is anything to go by will appear late on the scene and cost more than the estimates. (Fortunately the French are involved, so things may not be so bad.) Even so, by the time Concord is airborne, it would be surprising if there is no American Mach 3 transport in the production pipeline.

Are there any lessons that can be learned from this short survey of some aspects of the missile and aircraft industry's life? I believe that one or two important things about the reality of management come from these histories. The first of these is that monopoly power is not only to be feared when it is a protected producer monopoly, but also when it is a customer monopoly, and the customer is not under any real cost or other restraint. Like many of the other events and situations in this book, the relationship between the government and industry is a complex one, so that any necessary explanation may well be a little crude. The effects of the relationship can be summarized something like this. Given a long enough period of time, the relationship between the two parties tends to cease to be a commercial one related to economics and the market. The important managerial ability in its turn ceases to be whether or not a man is good at managing a business with all that this implies; it is pre-eminently whether his face fits, whether or not he is amenable to government functionaries and the web of contacts that are necessary when an industry has so many and so widespread dealings with its main customer.

Of course even governments cannot get away from the reality that progress usually depends on unreasonable men, and these too exist at the tops of companies. But generally the picture is one of people serving their companies almost as they would pass their time officially within the civil service. (It has its effect too in that aircraft company executives tend to stay put.) The relationship too has perhaps other important effects. The industry's dependence on government orders is so complete that it becomes subservient to its whims. The customer is *not* always right, particularly when he wants things at unrealistic prices. The record should by now have shown that you can seldom get products from the industry at original estimate price, yet regularly the charade of 'ordering' is gone through, the aircraft industry knowing that it will have to ask for more because the government's servants are unrealistic in the prices they ask, and the government's servants knowing they will have to agree because they do not know enough about the industry to be able to say whether or not the increases are justified, or whether the industry is efficient. As the system is organized, all this is inevitable. And it does not help to create an industry whose successes will be governed by something more than chance.

Chapter 6

Electronics: Commercial Failure

The electronics industry is the *Wunderkind* of the British industrial scene. One has only to discuss the problems of shipbuilding, textiles, or indeed any of the industries mentioned in this book to be met with a reply whose essence is 'Yes, but look at the growth achieved by some of our other and newer industries: take electronics . . .'.

So let us take electronics. Immediately we come to a major stumbling block. Almost everybody has a different definition of what electronics is. To talk of electronics as an industry is in fact misleading, for the production of electronic equipment is spread across a number of associated industries, and though the bulk of it comes from firms in electrical engineering (and some from groups whose major interests lie elsewhere: food, aircraft, hydraulic and mechanical engineering), yet much of the most interesting work is done by companies whose interests are largely electronic. Yet what is electronics? Is it the production of transistor radios and television receivers? If so, the industry's future is likely to be a bleak one, for most manufacturers of these are in truth assemblers of components. The research is largely done elsewhere and for other purposes, even if that elsewhere should be part of the same group. The reasons for research in this case? Defence, nuclear power, automation. These indeed are the electronic pace-setters.

This gives us the key. The electronics industry which is discussed as a growth industry is really an intermediate one. The products of this industry are generally seen by the public as parts of something else, usually capital goods. The components, whether they be single transistors or complex process-control lines, are put to use as parts of something which is only indirectly for sale to the public. The direct consumer bonuses come from the application of these to the products which the public buys, and in developments from this area themselves directly applied to the products. But hindsight shows that the growth of the industry has been both rational and irrational. It has been rational in that much of the industry's diverse production still comes from the large electrical engineering combines. This is not simply because electronics stemmed originally from electrical engineering (though the point of departure may now be very far away), for much of the growth of these companies has itself come from purchase and not technical growth. It is due too to the need of these companies to protect their interests in an allied field, and to the production and sales demands made by such products as radio and television, often requiring mass production methods and large amounts of capital before production can be possible.

The irrational growth has come from the side effects of defence and other government spending, which have forced companies into lines of business which they would not otherwise have willingly undertaken if the motivation had been one of profit to be made under commercially competitive conditions. This has in its turn led to some quite fascinating product mixes. Indeed in cases such as A.E.I. it is doubtful if anyone would consciously plan to have such a wide range of production if, say, they were starting the business *now*.

Progress across the industry too varies. Irrespective of age, some companies are more go ahead than others. Thus for all their size and history such firms as A.E.I. and English Electric, with between them some £400 million plus a year in sales, have not been able to achieve the dominance here of such comparable companies as Philips of Holland or Siemens of West Germany in their countries. There is an innate caution in the management of our large electrical firms which seems to stop them taking the mental leap required to say: if we are to have a widespread product mix, let us at least ensure that we make as much use of it as possible. One of the fascinations of electrical engineering and electronics is that so much is dependent on the quality of management. The industry is really a growing one not just in volume but technically. The bounds of the possible are as wide as managerial and technical knowhow can make them. For, particularly in some electronic fields, companies make their names and fortunes with products which were not previously in existence to markets which did not know they wanted them until the industry came along. Thus, given the expertise and capital, a new management can – and does – work wonders. Among old-established firms, Standard Telephones & Cables for instance (a subsidiary of America's I.T. & T.) was for many years acknowledged to be the least commercial of firms in the communications business. It made its main money from telephones and long-range communications equipment, dealing much of the time with the quiet lifers of the Post Office. It was a large infeed organization with an evident mistrust of vulgar commerce, for it made almost everything itself, whether this paid or not. Along came a new managing director and his team, and slowly but surely observers began to notice that S.T.C. were beginning to concentrate their activities in fields they knew best, expanding, and at the same time beginning to buy in components even though they might once have made the same things themselves.

This was an old firm fighting back. Whom were they fighting? They were up against relatively new U.K. entrants, both British and foreign. For when we turn to the real backbone of the electronics industry, there are some surprises. The great names are not only the Marconis, Deccas, and E.M.I.s, they include too some newish names – such as Ferrantis or Elliott Automation where British and American knowhow have been blended in a most carefully planned operation which has interests right across the electronic side of automation components and computers, as well as doing substantial defence and aircraft business and research (over 2,000 employees out of a total of over 12,000 plus). It is, however, a British business. What of those which are not? If one wishes to prove the twin theses that we are not at our best at innovation, and that where we find an exception it is usually run by technically qualified professionals, we could do no better than look at electronics.

The largest component manufacturer in the country is Mullards, a subsidiary of Dutch Philips. The field of digital computers contains not only I.C.T., much of whose computer production and sales are of American origin, Ferranti, Elliott's, and English Electric, but also I.B.M., Minneapolis Honeywell, Remington Rand, Burroughs. These last four are American. Indeed I.B.M. is more than twenty times the size of the entire British industry, does something like sixty to seventy per cent of the total Western European business, and alone has produced five or six times more computers than the number installed in Western Europe. (It does not of course do business on this scale here, indeed the American companies between them have probably sold no more than half the computers installed in the country – though they have sold a lot more by value). When one turns to analogue computers, a much smaller field, one finds that it is dominated by E.A.L. and Solartron, with many small firms involved in analogue units. E.A.L. however are American, and with one computer (Pace) have done more business than the rest of the industry together. Solartron? This is an almost textbook example of post-war British innovator's initiative. It is now controlled by the Schlumberger Group, which too is American. And in the field of transistors and semi-conductors, the survivors who between them carve up the majority of the market are again Mullards and a firm called Texas Instruments, which is, inevitably, American.

Now if you compare the list of directors of any of these foreign companies with those of their British controlled opponents, you will be struck by the difference in qualifications. The foreigners almost as a matter of course have some qualified people on the board, whether or not they are British (they usually are). Companies like Plessey on the other hand can it seems exist without them, though they make up for it by enrolling retired politicians. Plessey, of course, is a very special case. It is a company which has been content to make its living mainly by using other people's knowhow, and its research expenditure and facilities were for a long time thought to be small. It is fair to say that this is a situation now being remedied. Plessey, according to their last Annual Report, now claim to have some 4,000 people engaged on research and development. Even here, however, it is quite likely that the government pays for a large part, for government money now accounts for something around two thirds of the U.K. electronics research and development expenditure, and Plessey obviously get some of it. The money is channelled through the Ministry of Aviation, for Plessey are heavily involved in aircraft navigation and communications systems, as well as servo mechanisms and hydraulic equipment. They get more too through the Post Office as the Group is involved in research in electronic telephone systems through their subsidiaries, Ericsson Telephone and Automatic Telephone & Electric Company.

Plessey is not of course alone. Most of the large electronics firms are also heavily involved in government-sponsored research through work for the aircraft industry; and here we come to an interesting sidelight on research and development. The money mainly goes to British controlled companies. Now there is nothing wrong here, but what is important is this. Take away that money, and much of the effort now being put in would collapse. It would do so, however, only in these firms, not in what for shorthand purposes one can call the 'foreigners'. Though few concrete facts are available, inquiries in the industry lead one to the conclusion that, as in so many other industries, the foreigners (and one or two others) would continue research at the same levels whether government spending existed or not.

One must now, however, consider the foreigners simply in a United Kingdom context. They have behind them the resources of substantial organizations elsewhere, and in the American cases can in effect call on the results of research which has been paid for by American defence funds. American support is both quantitively and qualitatively greater for its industry than is ours, and the research tradition within companies is much stronger than it is here. Is it any wonder that the Americans here have been able to grow so rapidly?

We cannot as yet leave the subject of research; indeed we may now discuss it more generally. It is easy to justify such a diversion in a chapter devoted largely to things electrical. There is hardly an industry in the country which at some time or other does not have to call on the electronics industry with problems to be solved. (This in its turn tells us quite a lot about the place of electronics in modern society.) We spent on research in 1961–2 something like £630 million. Of this money £385 million was provided by the government, nearly two thirds of it going into defence. Over half went into aircraft, while electronics and electrical engineering between them probably accounted for about one eighth. For an industrial country in our position, this is ludicrously little. It is easier to state where this money did not go, than where it did. As *The Times* industrial correspondent put it in a *Times Review of Industry* article in 1963: 'Space research, with all its ramifications, is supporting the American research and development effort at such a high level. Apart from the obvious channels, it has opened up branches of technology which are largely unheeded still in Britain. Among them are rocket fuels, new metals, extreme refrigeration, solar power systems, even the large-scale cleaning of equipment to achieve clean conditions in dirty surroundings. Such benefits have of course to be equated to cost. In many cases they may not earn their corn in the commercial world for a long time to come, but they are money in the bank.'

If we turn back to electronics, however, we can narrow down the fields as yet hardly touched. Also out in 1963 was a private report of the British Institution of Radio Engineers. This states that there was a lack of direction and coordination of research endeavour in industry, and that the fault was partly the State's. It pointed out that there was little work going on in such fields as ultrasonics, radio propagation, network theory, and colour television. And just for good measure it went on to say that the volume of research in electronics was unbalanced and inadequate. It finally recommended a radio and electronics coordinating council. This might well save unnecessary duplication, as well as providing a chance to get some of the as yet little developed fields actively worked.

It will by now have become obvious why they are not worked. The same report also mentioned what it called the fashionable subjects on which work is done, low-temperature physics, plasma physics, and radio astronomy. Why are they fashionable? A research programme is not something which can exist separately from the manpower, money, and resources in hand. We bemoan constantly the lack of scientists. We should do well to bemoan our lack of top-flight electronics engineers, for in comparison we are extremely well off in such fields as nuclear physics. Much of our research then has been dictated not so much by our needs but by the manpower available, its training, and its temperament. Is there any more basic reason why we should be in this position? It is perhaps the easily observable one that it is more respectable in the social sense to be a pure – or nearly pure – scientist than to be an engineer. The British public has always had a picture in its mind of a scientist as a somewhat dotty, absent-minded dabbler in abstract thought, much given to beards, forgetting what day it is and well in the tradition of court jesters, clowns, and eccentrics – in the same sense almost as it views its Anglican clergy. On the other hand engineers have no such social standing. It is this which during the post-war expansion of education has led to this imbalance, and has further led us to take up research unlikely to produce results for many years at the cost of developing further substantial bodies of existing knowledge. What we have then, it seems, is pure research without thought of commercial profit on the one hand, and defence-sponsored research on the other. Both are largely paid for by the government. In between are a handful of professional or foreign-dominated companies who understand the value of research and development, while the great mass of industry does almost nothing.

This has yet another effect. It is the real reason why so many of the firms in the industry are no more than assembly shops, and like all such companies, not very securely established, even though their turnover may be large. This leads to an almost continuous production see-saw geared to home economic policy and conditions. Again we must be careful in our generalization, for as I have tried to show not all companies are like this. The electrical-electronic engineering complex contains some of the most aggressive companies on the British scene. It is these which have forced the production index for the industry well above that of industry generally. The record, however, is spotty.

If one goes back to the Barna thesis, one finds that U.K. imports have over the last few years risen much faster than exports. The world's former net largest exporter of electrical goods now ranks number three, after West Germany and the United States. Who is losing the business? It is the U.K.'s heavy electrical engineering companies, though comparable companies in countries such as Italy are increasing their overseas sales at a considerable rate. To take another example, British exports of power plant increased by nearly 40 per cent during the years 1950–61 to around £67 million. During the same period West German exports increased by around 1,000 per cent! It may be retorted that the periods are not comparable, as West Germany in 1950 was still artificially depressed as a result of the war. Yet one can still find that the Germans show a comparable export cash increase during the one year 1960–1! One cannot even argue in favour of the British industry that it was busy serving the interests of a heavy home power programme, and one national customer, for in fact the French situation is comparable. France too has one main national customer, yet the export record of the French industry, though smaller in scale than the German, is yet of near equivalent percentage order (though not in heavy equipment, where the modernization programme has for years taken up most of the industry's capacity). What this illustrates of course is simply the scale of effort.

What future is there, then, for the electrical engineering industry? Again we must go back to our differentiation between electrical engineering and electronics (even where the two are currently almost inextricably linked together within companies). Where the State is the customer, as in the electrical supply industry, we shall either have to put amalgamation and rationalization pressure on (this side of the industry after all is well used to working together, both formally as in the nuclear power consortia, and informally: the share-and-share-alike routine which is the rule in major power projects is a good example), or see some of the companies eventually go bust.

In electronics one can expect that economic pressures in existing fields will have the effect both of driving some assembly shops to the wall and of making others specialize. The field of automation, after all, is going to make considerable demands on the industry, much of it being small-scale demand where the little firm is in a good position. Almost everyone talks of automation in the sense of millions of pounds' worth of equipment in one plant. In fact, the major job that needs to be done is found in thousands of small companies, where what is needed is not the automation of the full production line, but the modernizing of the parts of it which can be treated on this basis.

Finally, if we are to accept the role of the State as a major customer and the major provider of research funds as a permanent state of affairs (and currently there is no other possibility) the industry will have to accept continued government pressure and inquiry into its efficiency and costs. He who pays the piper should be able to call the tune. It is a reflection on our way of running things that this is currently impossible: we do not have machinery available to make it otherwise.

Chapter 7

Engineering: The Failure to Rationalize

Most of this book has been taken up with the events of the last dozen or so years in certain specific industries. We have not as yet discussed the complex of industries which go under the general name of engineering – making cars, ships, commercial vehicles, chemical and other plant, aircraft, marine or other engines, and tools of all kinds. Any area of skill which has so many applications cannot of course be observed in conventional terms, for though the same basic skills may be at work they are spread over such a wide diversity of production and markets that they are extremely difficult to link together comprehensively.

To start any examination of any part of these industries – I have picked on cars – however short, demands a look first at one of the essentials of the industry's life, the basic material with which it works: steel. I renounced a proper examination of this industry at the start of this work, for in the export sense the steel industry is not directly a growth one. However, as the conditions under which it operates and its production very much effect the engineering industries, I need to say something. The steel industry should really be held up as a shining example of our inability to think *big enough*. We had in 1961 a production of crude steel of 22 million tons, with Britain the world's fifth largest producer after the U.S.A., U.S.S.R., West Germany, and Japan in that order – and soon to be overtaken by France. Our production came from some 300 firms, over 80 per cent of it according to the British Iron and Steel Federation from ten companies between them employing over half the industry's labour force.

Our dependence on steel is easily illustrated. The same source states that some 35 per cent of the industry's output is exported directly and indirectly, and that steel and steel-using products accounted for 55 per cent of total British export earnings that same year.

What this source does not state, however, is that we have not got all our thinking right. For though we are one of the world's major producers, and have been in the business actively longer than anyone else, most of the running is now being made elsewhere. What we do have are too many small units making a too costly product, when the shape of the modern steel industry demands large-capacity plant both for quality's sake and for reasons of economics. What we have and hold out as the best example of British steel skill is Richard Thomas & Baldwins' recently opened Spencer Works – where capacity is eventually expected to grow to seven million tons. It is not however just available capacity that is important but the percentage rate at which it is used. As in chemicals, the economics of large plants are such that the bigger modern plants produce a cheaper product, and one whose quality is more accurately controlled. This in its turn is of vital importance, for modern technology demands materials made to exact specifications. Large modern plant will give not only the cheapness of continuous quantity production but also controlled qualities. As things stand, there is no British steel plant among the world's top ten, or even twenty. For those you have to go to the United States, the U.S.S.R., China, and Japan. Even with Spencer Works, we shall still not be up with the European leaders, for there are at least five plants in Europe likely to be expanded to the same capacity at around the same time. At least three of these are more modern in conception and the managements have shown even more economic foresight.

The problems of large plants are many and complex, and are not confined solely to internal matters. Large capacities demand handling facilities on the same scale. The industry, for example, can take no comfort from the lack of handling facilities for the larger ore carriers of 60,000 tons and upwards which are going to be an essential for coast-based plants. Spencer, of course, is not coast-based. The political decision which put this hot strip mill down in South Wales seems to have been inspired by a lack of economic foresight (the industry indeed is not very good at forecasting. The 1957–62 steel plan supposed that we should have a steel demand of 30 million tons by this year; instead demand has been running at more than 20 per cent below this figure).

So Spencer works grows under handicaps. These are not however shared by U.S.I.N.O.R.'s Dunkirk project or the other large coastal complexes which have been built so that they are capable of further development many years ahead. Are large plants so economic? Certainly the people who have them believe so. Indeed I have on my desk as I write Russian published papers arguing the economic case for even bigger plants, and contrasting the economic performance of plants of 12 million tons capacity with those of 24 million tons capacity. These things are on the way. All this is well known outside these islands. Outside them too some experts believe that one of our major difficulties is the even more distressingly cautious approach of the steel companies to writing off. The correlation between the rate of write off and the growth of new capacity is now well known, and is applicable not just to the steel industry. But well known or not, the industry here has over the years taken little notice of it.

This inability to think big or outside the conventions of the early 1900s can be seen in other ways. We have talked in terms of sales as an index of company effort. This is valid, but an even better guide – at least in the field of public companies – is profitability as a percentage of assets employed. (I say public companies for a good reason. The private company with no need to distribute large sums may on paper be earning much less than the public company, though its profitability may really be as high if not higher. All it does is to have a far higher rate of self-financed investment. It can do things without the need to maintain a reasonably uniform paper profit flow. Turn the same company into a public one and much of this ability disappears, unless of course control is so overwhelmingly in a few hands that the same results can, if considered desirable, be achieved.) It is this rate of profitability which has been dropping. Even so, the steel companies here come off very well in comparison to much of the rest of British industry.[1]

One of the major users of the steel industry's product is the car industry. It is almost a commonplace today that this industry, though still expanding, is not as soundly based as is desirable. But what, first of all, is the motor industry?

It consists of the six major manufacturers, Ford, a General

1. I am indebted here and elsewhere to some lucid booklets introduced by the F.R. Bentley Company who have done some most interesting comparisons with companies abroad.

What's Wrong with British Industry?

Motors offshoot in Vauxhall, the British Motor Corporation, Rootes, the Leyland Motors–Triumph subsidiary, and Jaguar (who by volume of production can be classed with the major manufacturers). Apart from these we also have Rolls Royce, Rover's, the David Brown Organization, and a few smaller companies. Indeed, almost alone in the western world (the only exception being Italy) the United Kingdom finds it possible to support a number of smaller quality manufacturers able to beat the big boys at their own game. This tells us quite a lot about the state of the car industry (though one should be particularly careful of generalizations as standards vary enormously). What it tells us is this: apart from Jaguar, British engineering prestige is carried by the small production units, not the big ones. We are indeed in a position where the small companies continue to encroach on the major ones simply by sheer quality of product. The big company retort is interesting. It is not to raise engineering standards, but to increase the variety of production. In fact the industry produces more types and variants in proportion to its size than any other – with of course an effect on its costs.

The industry is generally acknowledged to be a growth one. I must, however, differentiate between total annual vehicle production and the number of firms engaged in the industry. I have written about the lack of desire for change in other industries. This applies too to car manufacture. Thus manufacturers have been slow to break their dependence on outside components suppliers. The trend to ownership of such firms has been going on for a very long time.[1] Ownership, however, is no substitute for integration, and much of the industry's production as a result is based on a finely balanced transport operation, itself dependent on labour relations, the ability of suppliers to produce and deliver on time, and the Chancellor of the Exchequer's temper. Again the results vary according to the calibre of the firm and its managements. In all cases, however, this has the effect of making the problem of quality control a more difficult one than it otherwise need be – apart from raising costs.

And then there is the problem of the number of unions involved in the car industry. There are of course two sides to this. First,

1. Though it is worth pointing out that much of it cannot be taken over and rationalized. Again foreigners have made a near corner in some of the industry's more profitable parts: i.e. Borg-Warner, Champion.

managements, as at Fords, can be incredibly ham-fisted, and the lack of communication up and down (largely because no one is quite sure whom to communicate with, and even where they are sure most of the people on the list have no authority) is enough to nullify the effects of any policy, however well intentioned. Second, whether Mr Cousins likes it or not, we already have the worst aspects of a one-industry union situation, without unfortunately any of the benefits. Let us look quickly at the one-industry union situation. (Anyone who does not believe that it can and does work should take a look at the labour records of the chemical or glass industries, which are nearer to a one-union situation than any others.) What makes it so attractive? For a start if there is going to be any trouble, it faces management and labour directly, the spokesmen for each being able to speak for what they think is their side, knowing that they are supported. Secondly, it puts a stop to the incredible situation where the effects of a hangover on half a dozen men can lead to some hundreds or thousands being laid off. It leads too, to the Walter Reuther situation where the one union is strong enough – and correspondingly rich enough – not only to be able to obtain the best brains but also to make use of them. The American union knows in considerable detail exactly what is happening in its industry, and is powerful enough to demand its share of any extra profits going. It is able, too, to take a much closer look at fringe benefits, working conditions, and many other sides of life which our people cannot.

That we do not have one in theory, however, does not stop us having the next best to it in practice. What we have are shop stewards' committees which effectively exercise the local power across a firm – without unfortunately the restraints or the non-wage-packet benefits. Again this is not wholly true across the industry: the record is mixed. The companies which in practice recognize the power situation that exists, and who take advantage of it (in the sense that the shop stewards' committees are their first concern), often have the best labour records. Those accustomed to a more formal structure and unwilling to recognize the facts of life usually have the worst.

The labour situation has other effects. It distracts attention from other problems. There is still too much of the 'This is casual labour' approach in the industry, and most of the welfare schemes compare badly with those found in firms of a similar size elsewhere (indeed, compare badly with those of its foreign competitors: Fiat, Volkswagen, Renault, etc.).

Finally we come to the future shape of industry. It is now a cliché that there are too many mass-production car plants in Europe for the size of the market. This is the real reason why profit margins are no higher. No one as yet has had the nerve, resources, or ability to lay down economically large enough plant – except on the continent: i.e. Fiat and Volkswagen. The result is that car-industry profits are pitifully low. The trend to small cars (where as things stand profits are even smaller) may well put economic pressure on some of the larger companies and gradually eliminate them, or again force more amalgamations and eventually larger production units. (It is after all an old motor industry truism that the possibilities of economically running a plant above its theoretical maximum capacity are very limited. However it is possible to run one down to seventy per cent of capacity and still not suffer a loss.) Fewer bigger units would not in fact reduce customer choice; they would enlarge it. For what we have now are vehicles produced by separate companies which differ from each other – envelope apart – only on points of details. There will always be people wanting different cars, and prepared to pay for them. A situation where two or three mass producers competed for a mass market might in the end accelerate the industry's introduction of new models. We should then not be in the position of having first developed a turbine car here, but allowing the American public to be the first to drive one. (The industry's rate of technical change is not exactly dynamic. Most of the so-called new technical innovations introduced have usually been introduced elsewhere years before.) The motor industry indeed provides a good example of a sector of the economy with too much slack; a slack which is only slowly – too slowly – being squeezed out. For too many units producing too small quantities of theoretically mass-produced cars can have other effects on the economy. Too small a plant means that production will not be as automated as is technically possible – or as would be worthwhile if the plant's capacity were larger. In the short term, it can be cheaper to use relatively unskilled manpower – which in slack times can be laid off – than to automate. (Another reason why labour relations in the industry are so bad. You treat people as casual labour, and you get casual service. The car industry indeed provides a very good example of the nonsensical approach of much of British management, found particularly in the engineering industries, to its labour force. Some are staff – protected, treated almost as management; others are workers – and no one needs me to tell them what that entails, though it would be almost impossible to decide who is more valuable to the firm.) The putting down of modern plant of modern conception requires large capital sums which could be justified only with larger production units with a far higher degree of integration of production than is now normally the case. The often publicly admired photographs of Britain's motor industry with their flow lines and hundreds of men milling about are themselves revealing. Many of the jobs they are doing could be done much more efficiently with a lot less manpower and more plant. Those men have a further effect: The major user problems with new cars are usually a result of a lack of standardization in make up, assembly, and finish. This often happens because the industry is using manpower for jobs which should be done by machinery – which will give you the evenness of quality that you want, whatever limits you may set it at. And then there are the side effects. Dispersal of production, too large labour forces for the productivity involved, a wide range of jobs, and differentials based on marginal differences in skills can lead to almost constant snarl-ups and lay-offs across the industry. And yet these stem from too small plant, which in turn helps to cause a smaller profit, which in its turn inhibits the capacity of the industry to rationalize, and so on almost *ad infinitum*.

If, then, the steel industry is an example of one area of activity where we are unable to think big enough, the car industry is an example of the failure of admittedly large-scale industry (by British standards) to think clearly enough of the favourable consequences which would flow from internationally *really* large-scale operation. It is not enough to say that it is a good export currency earner. Rationalized it could probably do much better.

Chapter 8

Rational Thought:
The Miracle Ingredient

So far we have in the main been concerned with some of the less fogbound areas of British industry and government. Most of the general points made apply with equal if not more force to most other industrial manufacturing sectors. There are of course some parts of British industry which have put up quite remarkable performances (though, I repeat, it is not a comforting thought that a large number of these are owned, controlled, or managed by either foreigners or immigrants). As a proportion of the whole of industry, however, the overall weight of these is small. Outside electronics and chemicals, companies with good growth records are to be found in some sectors of mechanical engineering, ceramics, spirits, paper, and in some parts of the food processing sector. These, while doing something to lighten a somewhat depressing gloom, cannot make up for the sorry disarray that the overall scene presents.

Can anything be learnt from the histories sketched out in these pages which could be useful in the future, as far, that is, as experience is ever of help in avoiding the repetition of past mistakes? I think we can learn quite a lot. This will not stop us making new mistakes, or give us solutions to all the industrial problems we may run up against. To paraphrase Kennan, we should be prepared to leave some problems for our grandchildren to settle. It should however mean that we shall not be faced again with the creeping paralysis which has been our major problem since . . . Well, since when? Some of the problems discussed in these pages made their first appearance in Britain around the turn of the century.

And here I come to the main point in this book. There are no easy, cheap, quick, or dramatic solutions to the problems we face.

We can attempt some bolstering and tempering operations. These will not be any substitute for what in the end will be a long haul – long in that the real effect of the solutions will be felt by what is now the younger part of the population, who simply because they are young are unlikely to reach positions of power for some time yet.

Anyone expecting me to call for either of those two intellectual dishonesties, wholesale nationalization or a return to an un-fettered free market economy, will be disappointed. In the context of Britain in the sixties, neither is the best solution.

What then is the best proposition? Not surprisingly it is con-cerned with government intervention in the economy. Govern-ment intervention of course already exists, and as I have shown much of industry is dependent on it. I do not necessarily ask for more, but we must see that what there is is more effective. Nor does it have to be specific large-scale intervention in the affairs of industry – most of the measures that need to be taken necessitate much smaller interventions than one would think, though their effect may well be considerably greater than the measures them-selves would indicate.

Before coming to this, however, we must first decide what sort of society it is that we want – and what are the limits of the possible. Any answer here must be subjective. To pose the question alone implies change. Almost everyone wants change, though there is little agreement on what sort of change there should be. One can see this throughout industry; almost every executive one meets agrees that industrial change is necessary. They may go so far as to admit that minor changes are necessary in their own business – usually those which will increase short-term profitability. The real changes are always demanded from other people: the government, labour, their suppliers, competitors, the rest of the industry. As far as they are concerned, almost everything in their shop is reasonably satisfactory, and there is little they could do to improve the situa-tion which is not in hand already.

What sort of change poses the question 'what is it we want to keep?' How basic does change have to be? Here I think we must get the priorities right and not be put off by talk of tradition. Most of the traditions whose coats are trailed across our view come from the 1800s, the period of so-called imperial glory. We hang on to them because it is this period that they reflect, not because they are of themselves of intrinsic value or commemorate anything of real importance. In fact, if we are to survive much of the change is outside our control. To have what we have decided we want forces us almost inexorably down one road. This is towards the highly skilled society whose real strength lies in its capacity to do things which other people cannot do. Obviously, though this means that industry has to be modernized, it does not mean that everything must be modernized. Panic measures to save high-cost backward industries are both a waste of money and a tragedy, in that people go on clinging to a future in a particular industry when it is known that the industry concerned has (at least as far as we are concerned), had its day. One has to be very careful here; the industry as it stands may have had its day, but this does not necessarily mean that the basic skills are obsolete. There is obviously little future, for example, in a U.K. spinning and weaving industry producing cheap woollens and cottons for export. The same industry producing high-quality, more expensive products from both natural and synthetic fibres is a different matter. What is likely to make high-skill industries survive, and kill off those without? The pattern of industrial development is the same the world over – and the direction in which things are going can be traced tolerably easily.

Country x becomes independent. Until then it has usually been dependent on foreign suppliers for manufactured goods. (I have roughly sketched this in Chapter 1.) It is a dependence, however, which they wish to lessen as quickly as possible, and so the State begins to force the pace of development – both for its own sake and to pay for imports. The really important imports, of course, are the machines and tools which it will use to start its own industries. It then begins to want to export part of their production to pay for more imports, and at the same time expands its industries, this time (this is, of course, a continuous process) going in for more complex products. Again we sell it plant and some of the components which go into the finished product. It then wants to export some of these products: The gathering of skills meanwhile means that it starts making the majority of the goods that it needs itself, and again it wishes to export these. All the time these products are the ones we make ourselves. The country then begins to go in for the manufacture of exotics; again we sell it plant. It manufactures these – learns how to cope with its own plant manufacture, and then wants to sell us both. To repeat then, we stay alive on this treadmill by staying ahead, and by manufacturing products that other nations will not get around to for many years. Otherwise we make some more conventional things better, and at such a price that it does not pay other people to try to copy them. (The best example I know of this is still Scotch whisky.)

The beginning then must be with an educational system or systems in the broadest sense. We have to so gear the system that it fits where it does – not by accident but by design – the possibilities open to us.

This is not the place to argue a detailed case for a wholesale reform of the educational system. I am concerned here simply with four aspects of it. First managerial training; second, the training of engineers and scientists; third, the provision of more adequate research and development facilities; and fourth, the training and retraining of industrial workers.

Managerial training: having argued in Chapter 2 that it is not necessarily essential, I shall now reverse my position and state that it is. Actually, this is not such a contradiction as it may at first seem. The argument in Chapter 2 was mainly concerned with the results achieved in three countries, France, Germany, and England, and made the point that in the post-war years the first two have grown remarkably rapidly, largely without managements which have received an academic imprimatur in the subject of management. It did, however, make the further point that the industrial leaders have grown on a managerial base the roots of which are academically acceptable. This is not the position here, and we must take the situation as we find it. There is no doubt in my mind that more comprehensive managerial training facilities would have helped us considerably the last ten years. The complexity of modern industry is such that managerial training facilities are going to prove more and more important. What do we mean by managerial training – and what facilities do we need?

It is obvious that the problem of managerial training breaks down into three parts. The basic training of executives to be, the bringing up to date with modern techniques of existing executives, and higher managerial training. It breaks down like this for one good reason. Though there is a lot in common to managements, the range of problems within industry can be considerable: the managing director of Company *a* may be unlikely ever even to hear of some of the major managerial worries which are the constant preoccupation of the managing director of Company *b*. The facilities we have are grossly inadequate. The British Institute of Management struggles along with a comparatively small subvention trying to do part of tasks number two and three by an occasional course, short period conferences, and the publication of pamphlets, reports, and books on management and its techniques. Tasks number one and two are also undertaken on an academic basis by such institutions as Churchill College. (Its first nine-month residential course for middle-rank managers in 1961 had fourteen students.) Also involved are the Foundation for Management Education (which has been instrumental in getting some University Departments started or expanded) and some of the Colleges of Advanced Technology. So far, however, the diplomas have little status or prestige, at least not in the same fashion as one hears that 'he went to the Harvard Business School, M.I.T., or Stanford'.

We should not let this present awakening to the need for managerial training facilities, which has also received the N.E.D.C.'s blessing, blind us to some further realities. First, we must begin to give more thought to what we teach. That a serious industrial journals should in 1962 still be printing articles on the fundamentals of operations research, or explaining critical path analysis, gives some idea of the need for instruction in the basic tools of modern management. Second, we must beware of concentrating too much on a school on Harvard lines at the cost of the rest of management education. The people who need educating are not only the successors; they are often – I hope by now that I have made this point – the managers of the present. A concentration on prestige high-cost schools would not unfortunately be of help to the many small firms who need trained executives. It is largely these who currently lack managerial expertise, and in them that top- and middle-rank executives need much more training.

Whatever training facilities we provide for executives, we are still left with the problem of the training of directors and top management. The main problem of top-management training can be simply stated: it is that there is no real substitute for the practice of management. All that we can do is to hope that the right men are selected. We must distinguish also between working and non-working directors. The only real test in business is success. We must therefore be careful to see that whatever reforms we make we do not set up just as dangerous an orthodoxy as the one we are trying to leave behind. One starting point in the reform of top management might well be to broaden public knowledge of public company activities. The current legal requirements are almost pitifully inadequate, and as things stand not even the government really knows what is manufactured in this country, or the conditions under which all goods are made. Making it a necessity to declare turnover, major cost breakdowns, export breakdowns, number of employees, composition of labour force, properties owned, and other assets at their true market value (among them interests in other businesses), trade agreements and their character, the net value of production, would make the area of public knowledge greater, and also begin to get some idea of company weaknesses. As this would make a temptation for the takeover operator to move in, it would, if nothing else, have the effect of keeping managements on their toes and give shareholders an opportunity to keep them there. It would not, of course, solve the problems of companies where financial control is in one pair of hands, or the hands of one family. Among public companies, however, it would possibly increase Stock Exchange speculation – which in Britain might well be a good thing.

A further step to reform might well be to take a leaf out of the West German book. A legal insistence on two boards, one supervisory composed of non-working directors whose main functions are to see that the interests of all parties are safeguarded; and a working board of directors in actual charge of the business. One can then bring in at the working level some form of expertise requirement. That in companies or groups of companies of a certain public value – judged by criteria coming from the published figures: assets, employees, turnover, or combinations of all these (the possible number of permutations is considerable) – a number of seats on the company board must be held by suitably technically qualified men and women who would go a long way to removing technical illiteracy in the boardroom, one of our major worries. It would of course have further advantages. It would help to introduce more promotion prospects for such people as production engineers and other technically qualified executives.

Screwing up the tempo of the rat-race for those who are in it would indeed have beneficial effects all round. It would help to break down the social model, and would of necessity also bring the academic world into much closer contact with industrial realities. We might even get to a point where a man would, again as in Germany, be proud to be 'Dr Eng.' or its equivalent, and where companies would also be proud to have such a man.

This takes us to the second leg of our four-part equation: the training and provision of more technologists, engineers, and scientists. This is a national problem demanding a national solution. It is however a twofold problem; first, how to train enough; second, how to make sure that they are, after training, spread throughout industry where they are needed, and not as now largely taken by the bigger companies who often are the only ones which can offer a worthwhile career. The first question has been argued over and publicly discussed at great length now for some years. We persist in the theory that the way to improve the situation is to create more and more Colleges of Advanced Technology, and expand such things as university engineering departments. What no one will really face is that we do not need hundreds of small schools spread up and down the country. What we do need are really large technical 'universities', with the facilities that large schools possess. Much of the strength of German or Swiss engineering is due to such schools. The Continental engineering training traditions, particularly in their social value, are much stronger than ours, and these schools – Aachen, Zürich for example – have for long been seen as of considerable national importance.

Presuming that we can obtain the engineers we need, how do we get them *where they are needed* in industry? We do in fact know where they are needed – the small engineering companies. We can get some idea of the need for engineering skills when we remember that, for example, the Metal Research Association – which is supported by the Department of Scientific and Industrial Research and can undertake considerable services for its members (many of which would be otherwise outside the small company's reach) – is supported by less than one company out of every five in its industry. We get some further idea when we learn that industry generally could be saved huge sums by the introduction of modern metal shaping techniques (I have heard estimates varying between £50 and £100 million annually). In most – though not all – cases, it is the smaller companies who are the main offenders against common sense. The creation of more managerial opportunity for engineers might in its turn make for a wider spread of qualified men. In the end it might create engineer-dominated companies, but this in itself, would be no bad thing – some of the major successes of British industry, Leyland's for example, are themselves engineer-dominated. I agree that one of our major difficulties is lack of salesmanship in many of the highly competitive high skill content product areas; but it is a truism that no salesmanship will ever make up for shoddy products, at least if the firm wants to come again.

Is there anything else we can do to see that we get the right men into the right places? One way might well be an industrial levy (something similar is going to be done with apprentice training). That a firm helps to pay for the training of technologists might help to condition it to employ more of them. The effect would most likely be a temporary one, for after enough time the demand for engineers would come normally.

It is not just production engineers pure and simple that are needed; we also need to have more people employed in research. This brings us to our third point. I suspect that we shall have to begin to use some form of compulsion to make companies do research – in the sense that either companies spend at least an agreed minimum percentage of their income on research and development, or they are made to contribute the same percentage to an industrial research undertaking. The Department of Scientific and Industrial Research has possibilities here. What would happen in practice would be that the larger firms would as usual continue to do research and development work, while many of the smaller ones would find that their money would be pooled on efforts which would often be outside the resources of the small business. It would not of course be all small firms which would contribute. Many go-ahead small businesses invest quite heavily in research. According to Harry Miller in *The Way of Enterprise*, Radyne Limited, a 700-employee company manufacturing radio frequency heaters, for example, spends about 15 per cent of its turnover on research (though Magnavox, one of its American competitors, spends more). This is a high percentage in any British industry. The results justify it, for Radyne is a post-war creation and in our context a success story. For every Radyne, however, there are ten companies in industry who hardly know what the word research means.

We must also clear up what we mean by research and development – there are no agreed definitions for either financial or company purposes. The latest current figures indicate that Britain spends around 2·7 per cent of the Gross National Product annually on research, as compared to the United States's near 2·9 per cent. We are, however, trying to do nearly as much across the industrial board – with, as I pointed out earlier, some prominent, promising, and expensive omissions – something which is going to have to be rethought. The fastest growth rates have come from industrial specialization. The Swiss, for example, go in heavily for processed food, watches and instrumentation, pharmaceuticals, and transport and electrical engineering. They are not greatly involved in oil, plastics, electronics, mass-production electrical consumer products, or frozen foods.

On the other hand, we are involved in almost everything, except that we are not seriously involved in space programmes and research. (I exclude the comedy of E.L.D.O.) Given that a quantitative American level is outside our reach, is there anything else we can do? The measures I have indicated would go a long way to step up the money we spend on research. They would have the side effect that a company which has compulsorily paid out money to the D.S.I.R. or Research Association will tend to make more use of the information it receives. I doubt, however, whether it will be enough, for research and development are not an end in themselves, they must eventually produce something, even if only answers to questions we have not as yet discovered.

Equally important is the point that money is not enough. There must also be a concentration of resources. We could in fact produce more were it not that the largest research spenders are often those whose research is the most widely dispersed. This comes from a particularly British approach noted earlier: that large companies too often tend to diversify on the short-term profitability advice of accountants, and seldom on technical grounds. The A.E.I.s and G.E.C.s of this world seem content with minuscule shares of many markets rather than larger ones of a smaller number. A hedging of bets and a lack of willingness to take risks or decisions are possibly the besetting sins of most of the managements I have criticized. This finds another outlet in risks of another kind, those of technical innovation. The N.E.D.C. report points out that there are many developments being carried out abroad on which we have so far done little serious work – though it does not put it quite like that. Among them it names vacuum casting, synthetic rubbers (the rubber industry indeed is so unadventurous that the best it can do is a joint project in the south of England and one or two small pilot plants within individual firms), new looms, and diesel electric locomotives. (We have a long way to go before we have engines in service as good as the best of those operating the main-line services of French Railways, and many of those have been in operation since 1954–5.)

Research and development as concepts are of course closely linked to attitudes to innovation. This is something at which we are not very good. The pressures to innovate here usually come from government requirements which in turn almost invariably have a defence connexion. Jet propulsion, radar, nuclear power, these and many more were developed and proved largely with government money for a basic national need. It was only when the direction was clearly mapped that their conversion and development for civil use began to attract interest, investment, and pressures from private industry. Can anything be done about this?

Again I think the make-up of D.S.I.R. and the N.R.D.C. should be looked at carefully – to see whether or not we have the beginnings of a manufacturing complex here. Currently, N.R.D.C. develops projects and then licenses them out to private industry. In some cases it is instrumental in setting up companies to forward particular aims, as with Cockerell's Hovercraft. (In fact the basic hover principle was already known in America some years earlier. The General Electric Company had a working 'car' before we had got any system off the drawing board.) What we need to do is to force industry to innovate by simple competitive pressure. This already happens in some fields, notably electronics, where the American invasion has in its turn attracted many British companies who would otherwise, I suspect, not have bothered. It should be possible to create an autonomous corporation backed with State funds to take up, manufacture, and market some of the new inventions which would otherwise only see the light of day elsewhere. There is little reason why we should pay out foreign exchange to relicense for manufacture here things which were originally British developments, but which initially had to be made elsewhere. The creation of such a company would, I believe, have an interesting effect, starting as it would from scratch; it would not be tied by conventional production orthodoxies. (The Hovercraft, for example, would not have had to fit into conventional aircraft industry structure and would not have incurred comparable costs.)

This would be one effect. Another I expect would be that it might not in fact find as much business as now exists awaiting some form of real action. A corporation committed to taking up D.S.I.R.–N.R.D.C. technically and commercially approved projects would find itself with considerable competition for the same products from industry generally, for competition usually breeds competition. It would breed too a sense of urgency. Perhaps as important, it would create an impression that research plays a vitally important part in our future, recognized across industry, and by so doing it might encourage more of this country's real brains into industrial research. We have to try to make it more of a pleasure and a pride for a trained man to say that he works for Company x, and not as now have him say so almost shamefacedly for he knows he only joined them because he could not find a congenial university place.

All these plans, however, will be useless unless we begin to think more deeply, and act even faster, about the training and retraining of industrial shop-floor workers. One of the major barriers to industrial expansion since the war has been a grave shortage of trained skilled manpower. It is something which mobility of labour, in the sense we think of it, will not solve. We may talk as much as we like about industrial mobility and the ability of workers to go where work is. We forget to mention that one of the major handicaps to their doing so is the lack of basic industrial – as different from sector – skills in much of our labour force. I have in any case considerable reservations about the advantages of a mobile labour force to which, in our context, there are many objections. The concept of labour mobility is really American, and it makes little sense to consider this country in American geographical terms. We are a small island (with an area not even equivalent to Oregon or Wyoming, while Texas alone is almost three times the size). It is true that much of America's labour force is more mobile, but who is it that moves? It is not the oldest established parts of the population in the long settled areas. It is the newcomers, the first and second generation immigrants, who are moving once more in a modern, more comfortable follow-up to the original pioneers. They are moving to such areas as Florida and the West Coast. Who imagines that they are going to move again – unless they are forced to do so? They are mostly going to areas where newer prosperous industries exist; going to put down roots. Granted that there is everywhere a part of the population go-ahead enough to shift. We have them too, but they are doing so already, to Australia, New Zealand, and Canada. The people who are prepared to move want, it seems, other things than those we can offer, such as a predictable climate, decent school facilities, a better working atmosphere, opportunities for advancement, and simple respect.

What we have left are strong local communities – which account for much of our stability, with unfortunately perhaps much of the adventurous strain bled out. Even so, these should provide a stable platform on which to rebuild our national industrial machine. Otherwise we risk aggravating the problems we already have. What then is the present industrial training situation? The facts are many and well known. I state simply the major ones, as a full account would make a book on its own. To become a skilled industrial worker it is seldom necessary to have done any proper course of training, passed examinations, or even, one executive I know maintains, be able to read and write. What you have to do is first to serve time in an apprenticeship (doing time would often be a better description). You need to start around the age of sixteen and serve for five years, at the end of which time there is no guarantee that you will know anything more than how to make tea. You will however thereafter be thought of as a skilled industrial worker in one particular trade, not a skilled worker in one particular industrial context, for these do not exist – even though the work itself in any rationally organized system would most likely cover a much wider range of activity than is now the case.

This would be bad enough if there were industrial retraining facilities available for those who need it. To be retrained however will usually mean that a man will have to suffer considerable financial loss, which in turn often comes at a time when he cannot afford it. It is not the young who need retraining; it is the older generations with families and similar responsibilities who have gone into industries which were then thought of as safe. Now, of course, they are not. The young for their part go in only as a last resort. Up in the north-east, for instance, they have learned their lesson watching what has happened to their fathers in shipbuilding. All the T.U.C. General Council can do is to talk of the inapplicability of the Swedish industrial union system to this country, while some of its members are disturbed that British ship-owners take their orders abroad. It is not, it seems, only the State and the Institute of Directors who need to be dragged into the twentieth century.

Is there really anything that can be done about these problems? All parties it seems are seized of them, almost to the point of *rigor mortis*. There is a good deal of talk, report after report, but almost no action. The only action so far recognizes that all these divisions exist, but in fact is not really action at all. In a White Paper published in 1962, the Government proposed to update the apprenticeship system only, it seems, if there is general agreement between both sides of industry. They propose a levy on the firms which employ but do not train workers – I mentioned this earlier – training boards for industries to decide length of training, the setting of syllabi, standards and tests, and the organization of courses. These will be financed from the levy and a government contribution. This is all right as far as it goes, and if it ever amounts to anything. But it does not really solve the problems of the later entrant to industry. In fact some companies (for example Leyland's) run training schemes for older entrants and have an apprentice class for what they call student apprentices, men who come in at eighteen or so destined not only for the factory floor but also for other branches of activity, sales, service, design, management. Leyland, of course, are not alone. Good apprenticeship systems exist in many of the large companies, particularly in engineering. They solve the problem of lack of examinations in a simple way: by selecting their apprentices from a large list of would-be entrants. They make considerable use too of 'day release', and are usually found working closely with the Local Education Authority. As Oxford and Cambridge in another context, these companies – Leyland, Rolls Royce, De Havilland – take off the cream: what happens, or does not happen, to the rest we have seen.

How did this situation come about? It is no accident that the firms with the best training records are those with the best social welfare records. Much of the rest of industry however still tends to think of its work force in casual labour terms (contrast the labour peace records of Vauxhall's and the rest of the car industry). The casual labour approach over the years has bred insecurity in labour, and the unions can be understood if they are as obscurantist as management in refusing to do more than pay lip-service to efficiency or talk of rationalization. It is here that the proposals for an industrial levy and industry-wide training programmes are important. What one must try to achieve is a position where direct company investment in its labour force is stepped up. It is noticeable that part of the reason for the good labour records of the social-welfare-conscious companies is simply this high investment in its labour force. Managements in this situation have to think hard and deeply (they probably also have good personnel departments. Personnel in this sort of firm becomes almost a key department and is suitably upgraded to attract the right men) before they get into a huff over minor matters. The pressures on shop stewards too are different; both sides after all have a lot to lose.

Suppose now that we as a society have solved the current problems of managerial, professional, and factory-floor worker training, and of ensuring that more research and development are done; suppose also that we have somehow or other cajoled, bullied, or simply converted the large mass of manufacturing industry to put the resulting skills and techniques to use (I am an optimist). Stripping away the basic social problems that still exist, would a solution to these problems be enough to get us out of our mess? The answer again is that it would not. There is one other area of activity that we must also consider. This is the provision of some sort of industrial framework which will in its turn bear some relationship to economic realities. And to do this, much of the conventional wisdom has to be stood on its head. Let me start by referring once again to the inquiry conducted by the Institution of Works Managers. They confirmed that one of the major drawbacks to efficiency was the insufficiency of standardization of production with its resultant short runs. This is something which is bound to crop up when industry is organized in small, often under-capitalized units, one of whose major hedges against economic worry is widespread diversification. (This is the position too of many of our large industrial groups. We shall turn to these yet again in a minute.) What do we do about it? First, we have to make it easier for the small go-ahead company to grow, though not too easy, for the competitive struggle has considerable advantages in that it breeds both experience and efficiency. One area in which considerable rethinking is needed is the provision of finance to small technical businesses to allow them to grow. We have nothing comparable to the Americans here, with their Federal Small Business Agency, a part of the Department of Commerce. The agency provides all sorts of help, particularly export. It operates in a social climate too where banks are as a matter of course interested in lending money. The American small business also, as a matter of course, goes to its bank for funds. Here? I have one case recently of a small businessman in a highly technical industry who is almost completely baffled by the mystique of the City and the conservativeness of bankers – and does not know where to turn for the funds he needs for expansion. His problem was a very conventional one, and it was easily solved. But this financial problem is a serious one for the small business, and it has its effect on making people spread their manufacturing net as wide as possible just to make sure the money comes in.

To return to the kind of society we want – and the kind economically possible. I have argued in these pages that one of our major problems is the smallness of plant (the cost has something to do with it. Our plant costs are often higher than those of our competitors, so much so that in the chemical industry, for example, many people believe that is the major reason why the big international companies seem to have written off the U.K.; why they have by-passed us and gone straight on to the Continent). We should not be too concerned about mergers of the same sorts of interests for the process of horizontal integration needs to be carried much further. What we should be concerned about is the process of vertical integration which makes the policing job that will have to be done that much harder.

The conventional left-wing fear of giant octopi has a lot of sense to it, but it should not be a general blanket condemnation of large size as such – this obscures the real issue. The powers of the government in the economy are now such that control of abuses by large firms should not be too difficult. And here some teeth need to be put into the Restrictive Practices Commission. What sort of teeth?

For a start we have to put the competitive squeeze on the large units, particularly those engaged in the large-scale manufacture of consumer products. We might make a start by making it illegal to operate not only price fixing but also price leading (the policy recommended by Lord Chandos. It is after all precisely the type of man represented by his lordship on whom the squeeze must be put). Price leading is simply a means of keeping down competition. Small firms who begin price cutting face the possibility that the larger firms will do the same thing to them, aiming at putting them out of business. The strong teeth here might well take the form of in this case dictating that selling below cost is illegal. (This does not say that selling below cost generally is out of order. A reporting procedure on individual instances would be enough in each case to start the machinery operating.) At the same time we need to take a fresh look at patent law. A situation has to be created in Britain whereby patent protection will only apply where a patent is actually used – the time span of the protection varying with the amount of use. We need to make it illegal for some of the more notorious process-killing operations to be continued, so that in every patent agreement a clause will appear which states simply that the patent has to be used within a given number of years or the agreement is void.

To return, however, to the problem of plant size. A Bow Group study (*Monopolies and Mergers*) early in 1963 produced a table of concentration in British study, the latest figures used being those for 1958. The table below is taken from this study, and shows net output in 1958 and the concentration ratio, or the amount of that production value taken up by the three largest companies in each sector. Far from the overall concentration being high, we find some surprising spreads of production in sectors which ought to be more concentrated.

	1958	
	Output £m.	Ratio (c)
Railway carriages and waggons	37	65½
Telegraph and telephone apparatus	36	58(a)
Insulated wires and cables	28	57
(c)Cycles and motor-cycles	16	57
Fertilizers and pesticides	23	54½
Glass	43	50
(c)Motor vehicles	194	47
Farm machinery	10	46
(c)Domestic electrical appliances	22	45
Industrial engines	21	41

	1958 Output £m.	Ratio (c)
Aircraft	118	41(b)
Electrical machinery	115	41
Office machinery	12	40
Textile machinery	20	37
Rubber	37	$31\frac{1}{2}$
Ships, marine engineering	84	27

(a) So much for a manufacturers' ring. As can be seen the real ring is much smaller than the P.M.G. approved association implies. What the Post Office has been doing here is restricting competition in the name of sleep.

(b) Before amalgamations.

(c) There is room to doubt that these ratios are in fact high enough. American figures available give somewhat higher ones. Even so what these selected figures show is that the concentration rate in industries requiring a large plant mass production or automated base is still too low. It is this in turn which leads to widespread diversification, short runs – for there are too many companies in each act – and the resulting inefficiency and high costs. A change in this situation, which is slowly coming, needs more general approval than it has so far received.

Larger plants will have a further effect too, on both management and unions. The right to strike will become a much more serious weapon in these industries, and its effect should be considerable as both sides will have that much more to lose if strikes happen. For these are industries which lend themselves to mass production techniques, even though the majority are not what we normally think of as consumer industries. (There are only three on this list, cars, cycles and motor-cycles, and domestic electrical appliances. The concentration process is working in the first two. In the third, the situation is farcical. The farce lies in the seeming contentment – talk of competition or no – with five per cent or less of the market that is held by some of the larger combines.) We need to be careful about a policy of concentration, for it is often the largest who are the sleepiest, and the biggest objectors to competition. If we are going to enshrine competition almost as a principle – which will be one of the effects (and in which we shall in any case only be following the example set by the European Economic Community in industrial matters. As eventual membership remains the declared aim of government policy, we shall only be making things easier for ourselves when we join) – we have a further task ahead of us; we must also take care to see that it is thereafter effectively policed. Of course there is no set concentration ratio which would be ideal in a competitive society. Such a society after all presupposes changes, and if competition conditions are to be properly enforced, it means there will be some people on the way up at the same time as others are on their way down – the normal state of man. If concentration of the kind at which many of the proposals are aimed can be achieved, and if we can effectively police it, there is no reason why the ratios in these tables should fall below the sixty-five mark.

What I should hope and expect to happen is concentration on the American model, where you may find three or four firms in an industry, each of which will have concentrated its activities on one area of production. Thus in diesel engines, there might well be three main manufacturers each taking one sphere of activity as its main line, say for example's sake a concentration on different horse-power requirements and the different markets. This would produce companies who took it as a matter of course that they would have a far larger share of the market than is the actual position today.

But how are we going to police competition? It is here that we return to one proposition put forward earlier: the area of public record has to be enlarged to enable shareholders in the first resort to have a chance. With this goes another proposition: the Restrictive Trade Practices Commission needs strengthening as to both staff and powers, and at the same time we need to see to it that the judicial procedure is speeded up – so that we do not have intervals of years before the challenge of a practice has a final decision. All these moves will lead towards the modernization of much of British industry.

So far we have been travelling somewhat conventional ground. But now we must begin to take wing, for modernization means automation, and automation in the modern sense is a revolutionary concept. It is revolutionary in the sense that it makes widespread increases in production possible without corresponding increases in the labour force. It makes the same increases possible indeed with much smaller labour forces. This is already on its way, for we are but a step behind America here. In the American electrical engineering industry, output increased by twenty-one per cent during the years 1953–61; at the same time employment declined by ten per cent. Similar changes are recorded in many other American industries – some of them with production and employment not so heavily concentrated in a handful of firms.

The same could happen here were it not that the British people have made it quite clear what they regard as the cardinal aim of government policy: to maintain full employment – or as near full employment as is humanly possible. Now, though few people may realize it, a lot stems from this demand, for much of the policy that will make economic and social sense is – as things are organized – diametrically opposed to a policy of full employment as we have it. Large automated plant and industrial concentration mean that employment in these areas will decrease, for what we shall be doing directly – though not necessarily nationally – is to put higher investment into plant and correspondingly less into manpower. This does not apply however to all industries, for much of our future lies in products with a high skill content which do not easily lend themselves to large plant, long production runs, or conventional automation. And here economic forces are going to work with a vengeance. The demand is going to be for trained manpower, with the few technically unskilled in the service trades. We are rapidly going to have to say good-bye to the days when the British were the laziest people in Europe, and this is going to hurt. The technological society means a wholesale revision of attitudes to education, in which the concept that a low I.Q. child is condemned to a life as an unskilled worker (or if he is lucky to leave school at the right time and live in the right place to be a skilled worker) is going to have to perish. Many of the skills that need to be taught could in fact be easily managed by people of low I.Q.s if the system was so organized.

The political requirement for full employment that the people have imposed on the political structure means simply that we are beginning on a path which will have incalculable consequences. (This in turn leads to another and more worrying question. Can we in fact have a technological society *and* the personal freedom which is this country's hallmark; or are the two mutually exclusive? I believe they are not – though I should be hard put to it to prove it. Fortunately this question is outside my brief.) A lot more stems from this political requirement than just making sure that the hitherto untrained get the opportunity to be trained if they are going to obtain work. We are going to have an industrially mobile labour force (in the sense that much of it will find itself obliged to look elsewhere than its present industries for work, not in the sense that it will have to move). I have argued, I hope strongly, against mobility in the sense that people have to move around this small island. The objections will become even stronger as automation really gets under way, for the physical problems of moving will be considerable. There is also the uncomfortable fact to face that those who become displaced will be (and are: see the present depressed areas) in any case the least fitted to survive – whether or not they move (this even if there was anywhere, either now or in the future, for them to move to). For the process of automation will not be confined to any one sector of industry or any one area; it will be applied in most industries up and down the country. We can bring in temporary palliatives to cut down some of these effects. We may for a start see an end to that cost pressure starter, unnecessary overtime. Longer training, the shorter working week, so that jobs are spread over a wider cross section of the population, earlier retirement, longer holidays (the U.K. has the shortest paid holidays in manufacturing industry in western Europe), all these things will help, and all except the spread of jobs are desirable.

Wherever we turn in these equations, we are always driven back to growth. Without substantial regular phased growth, there are no solutions. We know by now what is needed; what are we likely to do about it? Though the answer must be provided by industry, it is an answer that is dependent on government policies. Every child in the country by now should know of the existence of the balance of payments problem. Two reactions are possible in a time of crisis of this kind: one, export stimulation measures; two, restrictive home measures. In economic crisis after crisis, the government of the day has plumped for restriction, and protests have been shrugged off with talk of international agreements, Britain the world's banker, overseas confidence in the Pound, etc. What it really indicates, however, is a lack of nerve. One does not even need to pose the question 'whose lack of nerve?', for everybody knows the answer. We are blessed, if that is the word, with possibly the most uncorrupt government machine in existence anywhere. It is also the most cautious and ill fitted to cope with the modern industrial machine, for it does not have the men, the knowledge, or the organization to cope with the modern industrial world – let alone the pace of change.

What are we going to do about it? Before we turn to export stimulation we have to consider the government machine we have. It is for a start both overstaffed and understaffed: overstaffed in numbers, and understaffed in knowhow. It is this, so some of its critics maintain, which is the real problem when it comes to obtaining decisions before opportunities are lost. And yet, how can we have real knowhow when the machinery of government is itself governed by politicians who refuse to do anything more than tinker with the regulations made by their predecessors? Anyone who has ever looked at the complex system which the customs service has to administer will wonder why anyone does any export–import business at all.

It is not just cumbersome frontier formalities that one objects to, though these are bad enough; it is also the paperwork which needs to be done. The hosts of special conditions which need to be adhered to (the reasons for which the services administering them seldom understand) and the hordes of exceptions, special duties at special rates, and the rest of the cumbersome babu-mentality machinery. This can result in general obscurantism all round, and is often self-defeating. I know the case of one importer whose equipment imports carry a heavy duty unless they can be shown to be goods that cannot be made here. As, however, British custom is to sell the equipment without refinements, his parent firm gets round this by building in the extras! He does, he thinks, just as much business as he would if the provisions and the heavy duty did not exist. The same idiocies are found in export regulations. They do not stop business, they just make it more tiresome, time-consuming, and difficult. The strategic embargo list, for example, is a farce. If you have an order, you can almost always get permission to export anything short of nuclear weapons. Though, for example, the list includes some non-ferrous metals, in one sector one British firm did enough business two years ago with China alone to supply the needs of a large part of the Communist block.

It is not only the complexity of the system that leads to the lack of knowhow. It is also the composition of the services and the lack of the right form of expertise in the right place. The scientific civil service, for example, is handicapped both by lack of manpower and by lack of facilities. It is handicapped further by lack of people with whom to communicate. This has both fortunate and unfortunate results. The fortunate is that they can therefore get on with the jobs they do in their own way. The unfortunate is that their advice is not as often sought or taken as it should be.

And so we go on. Lack of expertise leads to the lack of provision of specialist services which I noted in my first chapter. It leads to ill-timed or ill-thought-out government interference without real plan, long-term aim, or cohesion. It leads indeed to Mr Marples and his wobbly cycle in the crowded, fast-moving, somewhat dangerous traffic conditions of London, a good description of the government machine in this modern world. Can we in fact do anything about this? The lack of expertise will have to be remedied, and remedied soon. For we share one problem with the rest of the industrialized countries. It is that though the area of government interest in the economy may not be expanding in percentage terms – in fact, it fluctuates – it is expanding in terms of cash and will continue to do so. It is becoming more obvious every day that the projects in which public funds are involved are increasing, not only in number but also in magnitude. We are past the stage when simple accountability to Parliament after the money is spent is enough. We need more control over the cash as it progresses through the economy, and we should have the right to demand that the money is used efficiently. In the case of defence funds, we have machinery in embryo already scattered throughout the service Ministries and the Treasury, for not all senior civil servants are ignorant of what has been going on. The existing rules of accountability have built up a substantial body of knowledge which needs to be put to more use. The Americans have learnt this lesson and learnt it well, as anyone who has recently done any American defence research or manufacture will know.

Presuming that we have built up a body of knowledge and expertise, and given it powers to service the government machine properly, is there anything else we need to do with it? We need also to give it the tools to do two jobs. First, cut down the number of people involved in the machinery of government; second, forecast the various possibilities that are open to us. Much of the disquiet in the country is not concerned solely with the lack of sense of moral purpose, for men in the end work out their own salvation, but with the lack of sense of physical purpose. The public in its own good sense is quite right not to take very much notice of the N.E.D.C.'s academic exercise, for the N.E.D.C. has as yet no place in the power structure. It may be that this will lead in the direction of meaningful national plans, and not the hotch-potch of possibilities open to us in various sectors: this might be all to the good. What is even more necessary however is to make the choices much clearer so that we are not left with two political parties each offering their own version of chaos, and each knowing that it cannot be otherwise for too much has been left to chance. Above all, we do not only have to give the Treasury computers and the rest of the electronic aids to forecasting, efficiency, and speed – we have also to teach it some economics.

So far I have hardly mentioned exports, except to mention the need for them, the types our living will increasingly depend on, and to point out some of the difficulties and some of the deficiencies on record. Is there anything we can do to stimulate exports which we do not do already? The current theories have it that the cause of the trouble is that we emphasize production at the expense of sales. The reason for this according to this school of thought is that too much of industry thinks that there is something wrong about salesmanship (which in the popular imagination too is all mixed up with sharp practices and haggling). This they think is an attitude shared by much of industry's top leadership, the result being that salesmen are seldom found in senior posts and that the field is not taken seriously enough. In fact the record of British industry is most mixed; some industries do well, others do badly. There are of course difficulties in the way of salesmanship. There is for a start the problem raised by Professor Barna which I referred to earlier. We do not sell goods in some of the fast growing fields because we do not make them, or make enough of them to have enough for export – for that is the way much of industry looks at exports. We do not sell in others (some of the chemical fields for example) because our costs are much higher than our competitors'. We do not sell in some fields because the firms concerned are too lazy. We do not sell some products largely because of the difficulties many small companies have in coping with the routines and problems (including here that no one outside this country may know that the companies exist for they lack overseas salesmen and agents). And we do not sell because often there is little enough money in it to make it worth the effort, because either costs are high or middlemen eat up most of the profit. And finally of course we do not sell because we do not take salesmanship seriously enough.

There are of course other reasons. Often we just do not know the requirements. More often than not – particularly on the Continent and in America – our manufacturers are just not used to the pressure of real competition. This does not mean that we cannot compete once we get used to the tempo of things. When some carpet manufacturers were introduced to the German market under Board of Trade sponsorship a few years ago, they were in a similar position to the girl in the song: 'It's her first time out alone among the gentlemen' – a little out of their depth. In 1962, however, they sold over £1 million worth on the West German market. It took a long time for them to get the measure of the opposition and discover that their quality and price were right, and that if they actually approached these 'beastly foreigners' they might do business; but they eventually tumbled to it.

Another story concerns a more complex product. The least European-minded of Europeans are the people of Luxembourg, a small but very prosperous country. Until recently Luxembourg was a good little growing market for British cars, one worth nurturing. On a recent trip there, however, I met three former British car owners who vowed never again. The troubles? Delivery delays, lack of spares, and lack of manufacturer interest.

Almost everyone who travels abroad on business hears stories of this kind, which do a lot to confirm the impression that when we talk of *caveat emptor* we really do mean 'buyer beware'. The natural reaction in this case is simply to look elsewhere. But of course some firms do take overseas sales very seriously. Their salesmen have expertise, speak the language, are backed by considerable facilities, and in the case of possible big orders the managing director himself will usually nip across when required to deal with special needs. We even have companies not averse to sending over their own aircraft to bring a prospective customer here to give him the full V.I.P. treatment. The test is, of course, that this sort of exercise works. Who works it? Not surprisingly the best records come from companies or divisions of groups which are headed by professionals. The list includes most of the real star names of the industrial scene.

What then can we do to make people push harder? For a start we are precluded from giving direct financial support to exporters by the GATT agreement – not by anything else (we need not take the Federation of British Industries' case against export incentives too seriously. The F.B.I. has for some time been fighting a rearguard action against government intervention in industry, including high rates of taxation, etc. They argue, too, somewhat fallaciously, that these are discriminatory and that they must be supported by a clear demonstration of national advantage). Given however, that some sort of competitive conditions have been re-created here, and that we are on the way to rooting out some of the glaring inefficiencies of industry, we can argue that a discriminatory tax system in favour of exporters, and a discriminatory credit rate (as in France) in their favour, would be of considerable assistance. Why not T.V.A.? GATT agreement forbids only direct financial help to exporters, not indirect. Within this latter group is the Tax Value Added system in use in France – and soon to be in use in West Germany – which the N.E.D.C. recommends. This is simply a system whereby the same tax percentage is added to the value of a product at the various stages of manufacture. The final manufacturer or exporter then gets the total tax refunded when the goods are exported (in fact he receives a little more, for he gets his final price percentage). The effect is simple: overseas prices can be lower than home ones withour incurring anyone's displeasure. T.V.A., too, has further advantages; among them is obviously an incentive to efficiency.

For let us make no mistake about this, we are now in almost crisis conditions. Capacity growth is not enough, export growth is the vital necessity. Overseas sales have to increase drastically over the next few years, for without this growth is meaningless. Yet we have to do this at a period when competition has never been stiffer – on top of all our other disadvantages.

These then are some of the industrial problems that would face us if we bothered to look. It is not only as Mendès-France put it that 'To govern is to choose'; choice is also the necessary condition of survival, even though we try to avoid it.

I do not believe that the story of these last few years represents the permanent face of Britain, or that the few measures I have put forward are the only or necessarily the best solutions to our industrial worries. Or even indeed that they would solve all the problems to which they are proposed solutions. We are, however, in the position that we cannot have what we want without changes likely to cause the same effect. We start – and let no one believe otherwise, for starting is what we are doing – with phenomenal advantages over many of our competitors. Even if we have been fooling about for the last ten to fifteen years, and our bad management has meant the shocking waste of human materials – badly taught, badly led, and morally bruised – we are still as yet in no worse position than our competitors. Neither is the same manpower any worse than anyone else's. Such fallacies should not be seen to be the object of this exercise.

We have an urban society; no serious underdeveloped area problems in the sense that they exist almost everywhere else. More important, the technological society moves ahead fastest where the technical basis of the modern state is part of everyday life and is accepted as a matter of course. Anyone who has ever seen 'ton-up' boys working on their motor bikes will understand that familiarity in this sense does not breed contempt; it is one of the requisites for industrial growth and industrial reform.

It may be, of course, that we shall not in fact accept the notion of gradual change, but instead prefer to go on in our old and our present sloppy ways. Certainly the history of these islands is in practice against the idea of gradual change, if the changes concerned are going to be drastic, in any case. The British, however, also have a reputation for leaving Rip Van Winkle's state every so often and getting up to clobber their leaders, political and otherwise. This is in line with the philosophy, if one can give it such a name, that the best protection a free society has is to be led for most of the time by incompetents. Once upon a time we could afford this, for after all no one confused the strength of the country with the postures of its more recherché leading figures. I do not believe that we can afford it any longer, and the chance that efficient rational leadership may in turn put strains and stresses on a free society will have to be taken. For a useful starting point, one might well ask this: is now perhaps the time when we should begin to bury our dead?

Postscript

The Macmillan Era:
Si monumentum requiris, circumspice

Much water has flowed since I wrote the bulk of this book: unfortunately it seems to have been a tidal flow and real progress has been minimal. There has been an upsurge in business and industrial activity, though there are few indications – one or two major industrial units apart – that the necessary industrial groundwork to make this more than a temporary phenomenon has been or is being done. (Overtime, after all, was never a substitute for efficiency.) We are still beset – to the same degree – with almost traditional cliché problems; amateurs continue to be succeeded by amateurs; the gentlemen-versus-players war is still with us; and though we now know a few more questions and answers, we still seem as far as ever from taking effective action.

A wealth of evidence about our national life in general, and our industrial life in particular, has been appearing in the last few months. We have had the Profumo affair. The leadership of the Tory Party has been touted around the country like a trading stamp concession (as the late President Kennedy once remarked, 'No politician really likes to be a whore, but I must say some are less reluctant about it than others'), and the fourteenth Earl of Home has slowly backed into the limelight and Downing Street.

We have had a flood of policy announcements and reports – most of the latter recommending drastic change at some time in the distant future. But what we are to get immediately – if anything at all – is the mixture as before, only more so. So the country is full of plans for the years 1980 or 2000. One could wish that

117

there were a few more realistic ones around for the years of the sixties.

For what we need are some serious answers to serious questions, and not, as we have been having recently, half-answers to half-questions. In future, we need to see that the Committees, Commissions, and the rest of the investigating bodies we set up are given realistic terms of reference. Take the Robbins Report on instant higher education. This has been surrounded by considerable controversy, and has come under attack particularly in *The Times*. There the line taken has been the one put by Kingsley Amis in *Encounter* some time ago: that more will mean worse. What this controversy has continued to exclude is the question not of numbers, but of the content of education. The best comment I have seen on the Robbins Report (to which it is doubtful if we shall ever receive satisfactory answers) was by Mr Eric Robinson, Head of the Department of Mathematics, Enfield College of Technology. He was writing in *New Society*, from which the following extract is taken.

... the Robbins Committee found little worth discussing about the purpose and content of education and devoted most of its time to status and organization. What is the primary function of a university – education or research? What types of education are appropriate to a university? What types of research? Why are these appropriate? What should a degree signify and what should merit its award? What is wrong with university teaching, research, selection, examining? *Above all, what sort of people and knowledge will our society need in the future and how can they be developed?* [My italics.] The answers to such questions as these should form the basis of a scheme for higher education in the future but the Report makes no serious attempt to deal with any of them. Indeed it almost seems to suggest that these questions should not be asked or answered. But the Committee's answers are implicit. We should continue as we are, but more so. Our universities are in the hands of excellent men who produce excellent men who must obviously meet the needs of society provided there are enough of them.

We are in our present situation partly because the system we have built up has not produced people equipped to lead our sort of society. (The best argument against the major public schools after all is not the one based on envy. It is simply that on any realistic look at the evidence, they do not provide the élite we need.) The Newsom Report *Half our Future*, which is of as great social import, has not received anything like the same consideration. Yet even if only a small percentage of the moves towards modernizing the industrial economy come off, we are going to need to turn that part of our population employed in manufacturing industry into a labour force in which skilled workers predominate. Though we are – again in a national context – still a long way from the push button economy, the place for the semi-skilled and unskilled is decreasing and will continue to decrease. Those not destined to climb the promotion ladder will require a better, and certainly different, education from that which it receives today, even if only economic reasons are considered.

But let us turn to things of more immediate and direct concern to industry. In the field of transport, the situation is becoming even more critical. Mr Marples (as the irrepressible Mr Leslie Hale once pointed out) continues to make orders about roads once every couple of hours. Meanwhile, Professor Buchanan has produced Mr Marples' long-term plan to shatter the country. Unfortunately the plan is geared to the motor car we have today; says little about the future of personal transport, though it claims to formulate an approach to problems up to the year 2010; and does not examine the car industry, its future, and its possible future products. The Buchanan Report indeed is a near classic work about the static society projected nearly fifty years ahead. Yet all our experience of this century (and the many recent reports, including Buchanan) tell us that a static society is precisely what we do not have.

Next, let us turn to the Rochdale committee and its report on ports and associated facilities. Where are the plans for the large bulk carrier facilities: the craft which are beginning to make economic sense for large scale importers such as ourselves? They do not exist; instead it seems we are going to 'modernize' willy-nilly almost every coastal hamlet in the country. The shipbuilding industry in a new surge of life based largely on State loans and government orders has recently obtained orders for (among other craft) large bulk carriers. Once they are launched it is unlikely that, on the basis of Rochdale, they will be able to call or dock here. And while we are on the subject of shipbuilding, where – naval submarines apart – are the nuclear-powered craft? They are still on or about the drawing board. Progress here too might have been faster if we had not originally settled on a design now known to be unsatisfactory. Meanwhile, Russian and American nuclear-powered surface ships are in existence, obtaining valuable experience; the Germans and the Japanese are building; and plans are far advanced in France, Sweden, and Norway.

And now to industry itself, first considering Britain alone. One of the most eagerly awaited of the many reports we have had was that which appeared last July, entitled *Engineering Design*. This came from a C.S.I.R. Committee under the Chairmanship of Mr G. B. R. Fielden. On the day it appeared, *The Times* Industrial Correspondent commented

The vein of trenchant criticism runs all through the report. It is understood that Whitehall only agreed to its publication with reluctance.

What did this report state? That our share of international trade in engineering goods had been declining. It went on that

there is evidence that the importance of design is not sufficiently appreciated by the managements of engineering businesses ... The effects of the shortage of qualified and talented designers are, however, shown in the inadequate use made of new engineering knowledge in the design of some of the traditional products of British engineering industry.

What is the total physical contribution of the mechanical engineering industry to our national life? Including much of the output of the industries we have already covered (particularly aircraft and cars), the engineering industries, according to the report, account for 35 per cent of manufacturing industry's contribution to the G.N.P., and for nearly half the total exports. The exports, in turn, are equal to about a third of engineering production. Fielden makes the point, with which readers of this book will by now be familiar, that though British exports have been increasing, international trade has been increasing faster. The report goes on to state that though imports of machinery (equivalent to 28 per cent of machinery exports in 1961) may still be regarded as small, we cannot regard with equanimity the increasing dependence of some British industries, and particularly British export industries, on foreign plant. It states that our direct costs, i.e. labour and materials, are unlikely to be lower than those of our overseas competitors, and that we can have little hope of achieving any advantages in final cost if sectors of our industry are using the same machinery and manufacturing methods as our competitors. It then points out that during the three years 1960–2 more than 25 per cent of the domestic demand for textile machinery, machine tools, optical instruments, and office machinery – including computers – was filled from overseas sources. The evidence given to the committee and studies made by the D.S.I.R. show too that there was a high degree of dependence in some industrial sectors on foreign licences (which is what happens when you don't do enough research and development, or do it in time), including those parts of industry involved with foundry equipment, marine engineering, some metal forming processes, and a 'very large amount of steel making plant'.

The Air Ministry is quoted on the high cost of unreliability in the Royal Air Force: 'Maintenance makes up 50 per cent of the total cost of the R.A.F. . . . Spares alone cost £100 million a year.' This in a section headed 'Use of Basic Engineering Knowledge'! Elsewhere it goes on, again about the R.A.F.: 'The primary cause of the high cost of maintenance is lack of designed-in-reliability and maintainability.' Fielden looks too at British standards, and finds not only that the B.S.I. is slow to revise or delete obsolete standards, but that in some important sectors such as machine tools (excluding gear cutting machines), pumps, and materials-handling equipment, there are no British standards at all.

Interestingly enough, of the fourteen recommendations made by the Committee, half were concerned with the need for education. Of the remainder, perhaps the two most important were concerned with the need to make wider use of development contracts to encourage good design, and the possibility that we might make use of State purchasing to insist on high standards. As the State is the largest home customer (and, as I have tried to demonstrate, it is doubtful if its machinery is fitted to cope with the second half of the twentieth century) this would be an extremely large undertaking. One need only think of what it would do for example, to upset the 'buggins turn' routine of so much government purchasing, in say telephones or electrical power generating equipment. The development contract idea has now gained some notable adherents – in spite of one or two noticeable flops. It is just as noticeable too that more government intervention in the working of industry is not just a trend which is being fought, but one also gathering considerable support. Thus the Trend Committee report on the organization of civil science wants to go further. It suggests setting up an organization to take on some of the neglected ideas that are available; one which would issue the initial orders to industry. It might help things along a little to give this organization power over bought-up but unused patents. We need, too, to put considerable weight behind the proving, production, and marketing of the many developments which will make the petrol and diesel engines obsolete – so that we, instead of other people, get the benefits.

I have argued earlier in these pages that making more company information available publicly would have an effect on the health of industry, and the climate of investment. This is a view for which there is now growing support: thus the President of Goodyear, the world's largest tyre company, on a recent visit to England, said, 'British investors are blindfolded. I don't know how they ever make any investment decisions. . . . Over here they must pick their stocks with a pin or something.'* We have had, too, Mr Harold Rose's study for the Institute of Economic Affairs and pressure beginning to come from investment analysts, whose job in present circumstances is not particularly easy. We may expect eventually that there will be more pressure from within industry itself – that is if Lord Franks's B.I.M.-sponsored proposals for a Business School worth the name are taken up. It is, after all, the trained who expect to be able to work on a basis of fact and not by the methods more akin to spiritualism or elementary arithmetic, which are still too often the norm.

Most of the problems which have been cropping up in this book are interrelated. That the relationship is not normally seen in the sort of terms people can understand is largely due to a lack of economic research. Any national industrial policy worth the name should be based on fact. But is it? The N.E.D.C. apart, government economic research is inadequate. It is not only the government one should worry about, however. According to a recent report from the Royal Economic Society, non-government (i.e. university and company) economic research cost less than £1 million in 1962, and more than a third of that went into agricultural economics. Said the Committee:

The most obvious consequence of the present inadequate scale of economic research is, in fact, the number of current problems of economic policy where ignorance of the facts, and of the relationship between facts, lies at the roots of error and misfortune. . . . Efforts to establish an incomes policy are having to be made with inadequate knowledge of wage structures and of the influences bearing upon wage determination.

* To Robin Purdue of the *Evening Standard*.

But what else can we expect when the number of economists in British industry working on economic (as distinct from specific market research) problems is probably no more than three to four hundred?

Let us look at these problems from another angle. It may be that the industrially depressed areas of the north are not in decline, but in transformation (as we were told by the recent White Paper, *The North East – A Programme for Regional Development and Growth*). Yet all the acts and measures so far made to develop, re-distribute, and modernize industry and the depressed areas have made surprisingly little impression. The rate of unemployment in the north has been almost consistently higher than the national average since the early thirties, even though migration from north to south has been heavy. And how indeed can companies be made to move into underdeveloped areas like this when the national rate of growth is not high enough for there even to be sufficient companies expanding and able to move? Where some expansion has been possible, as in the chemical industry, the north has had its share. (There are, of course, special factors here. Much of the chemical industry is in any case northern-based. For the industry often makes physical demands difficult to satisfy in the over-crowded south.) The north too has had its share of industries which should not be spread out and dispersed, if, that is, we are to approach anything resembling economic working. Yet we continue to talk in terms of the dispersal of industry almost on cottage craft lines. How long will it be, however, before the migratory trend of the most active parts of the population can be reversed? Because unless this is possible, any economically realistic modernization programme is not possible.

What changes – if any – *have* occurred in the industrial growth fields covered since I wrote the previous chapters? In the field of chemicals, the position is improving. The reorganization of I.C.I. continues. Not only are the divisions being grouped around production capacity, but I.C.I. is beginning to concentrate. Plant sizes are going up. In the last few months there have been reports that I.C.I. is going to install the largest ethylene producing unit outside the United States, and that it has on order the world's largest nitric acid plant. All this will continue to slim down the size of I.C.I.'s labour force. And it is not only I.C.I. The Distillers Company too are expanding, and Courtauld's have recovered from their shock and are also beginning to show a considerable growth largely based on increased production, productivity, and aggressive sales. In the background loom the possibilities opened by oil pipelines, which at long last we seem likely to get. The majority of these developments are of course still on paper or in the process of installation, and doubts that we shall catch up on our competitors are many.

In the electrical engineering and electronic fields, some progress is being made. In consumer items it looks as if the idea of 5 per cent of the market for each producer is slowly coming to an end and competition is beginning to be meaningful. At the heavy industrial end, G.E.C., A.E.I., and English Electric seem to be slowly rationalizing or temporarily getting together in some of the export fields (temporarily because in many areas one can foresee the weaker partner eventually being squeezed out). Otherwise the temporary boom seems to be largely due to a rapidly expanding electric power programme, whose current growth is due to faulty estimating in the late fifties. The most lively heavy equipment firm continues to be the G.E.C. which is beginning to set a competitive pace which will have many effects on the rest of the industry.

In digital computers, we now have three major manufacturers. I.C.T. now include what were formerly E.M.I.'s and Ferranti's computer production divisions. English Electric and Leo have merged, and Elliott's as yet have much of their end of the market almost to themselves. Yet industry is nowhere near receptive enough to their products, and much of their growth is still too dependent on service industries. Now the cry is for government help, even if it should not be more than a differential tax aimed at making industrialists install modern equipment. This last is an approach which would be of benefit in many other fields, such as machine tools where the need is to give industrialists an incentive towards finding out more about their own production processes.

The machine tool industry is still in the doldrums.

In the field of aircraft, the position is now becoming farcical. At the time of writing there is no new fighter in production. Due to a typical muddle, we are likely to go back to develop and produce an aircraft of the fifties which will again be obsolete by the time it is in squadron service. At the same time we continue to persist in an industrial *folie de grandeur* worse than de Gaulle's. No one *knows* what the TSR2 will have cost by the time it is in service.

The official 'estimate' of £400 to £500 million is believed not originally to have been an estimate at all, but a figure arrived at when work was already well under way. Even this very conservative estimate means that there will be a lot of money spread around the aircraft and electronic industries. (Much of it, incidentally, has already been paid out and helps to account for one or two of the recent good financial results of firms involved in the project.) Unfortunately the TSR2 gives every indication of being nationally unproductive. It is so complex and expensive that no one else wants to buy it at the moment – even if it works. (It may fly, but we cannot tell whether it will *work* until its main weapon has been tested – and no one knows when that will be ready, or if that too will work.) If ready in time, the TSR2 will no doubt be the most advanced aircraft flying, and the techniques it embodies will also no doubt prove to add up to money in the bank in later years. I have written earlier that we have been spreading our resources too thinly: the TSR2 project is a good example of what can happen when you accidentally concentrate without a clear knowledge of effects or objectives.

As for the rest of the aircraft industry, its future is as problematic as ever. On paper B.A.C. has taken steps to reorganize its manufacturing activities. This can be read in two ways. Either they are preparing for a cutback – in guided weapons? – or for expansion. One suspects the former, for already the VC10 orders have been cut, compensation has been paid, and there is a likelihood of further cuts in the offing.

In the missile and guided weapons field proper, the muddle and lavish expenditure of the fifties have given way to the muddle and parsimony of the sixties. The only real contributions to anything approaching missile technology likely to bring industrial benefits in the near future are to be found in four guided weapons now under development and production – none of them exactly in the outer-space class. For anything approaching this, we continue to rely on joint programmes with other people. The biggest of these is ELDO: Yet meanwhile, some of the other ELDO participants are themselves planning independent programmes, and we must sadly watch as another of our leads is thrown away.

In the steel industry surplus capacity, a temporarily more flexible approach to prices than our competitors, and an unexpectedly buoyant home market have covered up the slowness with which the industry is modernizing. More than most, the steel industry realizes the extent of its problems, and some steps have been taken to extend the production of special steels. But generally, the outlook is not particularly set fair.

In the car industry the big question is whether or not Rootes will survive the year as an independent industrial unit. The industry has been going through a boom. How long it can continue no one knows, for the boom is very precariously based. It hangs not only on home but also on a fickle overseas demand. Much of this growth has come from Western European demand, and could take a sharp knock if the war begins to hot up – as it eventually must. An end to R.P.M., pressure on the components manufacturers (partly as a result of the Monopolies Commission report mentioned earlier), or an unexpected styling switch as a result of American changes, and much of our over-extended motor industry could easily be in trouble. Structural changes are on the way, it is only a question of which events will force rationalization and when.

In terms of industrial organization, there have been two steps taken during the last few months likely to have major consequences. First, the announcement that we are to have industrial committees set up by the N.E.D.C., in many ways comparable to those operating under the French plan. Secondly, if the current investigations are successful, we may well see in the near future a new industrial organization in which the three existing employers' institutions (the F.B.I., the B.E.C., and the N.A.B.M.) will be merged. The first move could lead to a market 'carve up' – or even to the energetic eventually putting the rest out of business. In the long run it could be more effective as a regulator than anything we have so far seen. The second could enable employers to face the government (and the unions – the effects of this on union structure and membership, given a fight or two, could be dramatic) united – and possibly mean an end to the present system which encourages the government machine to play off one against the other almost continuously.

It may also allow the expert industrialist to bring more pressure to bear not only to make the government aware of the problems and benefits of automation but also move them to take some necessary action. For the problems of automation are going to be the crucial ones that we shall have to face during the next few years. At their 1962 conference the members of the Institute of Directors were told that they were largely to blame for the loss of our lead in automation: that automation was not going on as fast here as in other countries. Yet it is currently easily possible to delete a million jobs from the British economy without difficulty and without impairing the G.N.P. Indeed to so so would probably greatly improve efficiency, lower costs, and help to strengthen our competitive position. But how can the industrialist – even if he knew – really move? The problems caused by automation are really political. We do not have enough jobs or realistic resettlement or retraining policies. A wide spread of automation however would make these even more necessary; without these, in fact, no government stands a chance of being re-elected.

The scale of change that automation involves is best recognized in America, where there is general agreement (I take it that an alliance of the President of the equivalent to our T.U.C., the President of one of the largest steel companies, and Henry Ford could be taken to mean general agreement) that a national policy is essential. Perhaps the major assumptions that will have to go overboard are that training is a once in a lifetime thing, and that many of the so-called skilled jobs could not be done by later entrants, or people of a much lower intelligence. After all, we manage to retrain the handicapped, a far more difficult task. The only real problem here will be one of scale.

The problem is compounded by the political reality that Mr Harold Wilson has nominated automation as the great problem of the near future, and anything that Harold Wilson says cannot be regarded as suitable for a Conservative policy. (Dishing the Whigs I am afraid is no longer much in fashion.) But what we must begin to realize – it has been obvious long enough – is that many problems now have not party solutions, but simply solutions, and it does not particularly matter what labels are put on them.

Alas, any close look at the evidence of the last few months still shows that our Continental friends are smarter than we are. Of course, anyone who has had such a look knows that this is not really true. The Dutch, French, Germans, and Italians can be just as lazy, mixed up, or stupid as we are. They too have serious problems of their own, and they too can feel that no solution can appear within their own generation. Yet in the mainstreams of economic life, they continue to be successful.

These successes have many sources, prime among them being a

recognition that drive is not something to be automatically impeded, that you don't get anywhere without vision, that the best place for the old and tired is in retirement, and the best place for talent is at the top. Here? As the Duke of Edinburgh recently remarked – and even he cribbed it – 'There are still too many one-ulcer men in two-ulcer men's jobs.'

January 1964

Index

Index

Index

Two other Penguin specials are described on the following pages

Two other Penguin specials are described on the following pages

What's Wrong With Hospitals?

Gerda Cohen

It is generally recognized that our hospitals offer a fine medical service. But patients are human beings, as well as 'cases'. Does consideration for the individual in hospitals match the medical treatment?

Gerda Cohen set out to find the answer to this question. She toured the country, talking to administrators, doctors, matrons, nurses, and patients in both medical hospitals and mental institutions. Her book is a highly personal account of what she discovered. In addition to the many impressive advances she noted, there were many things that shocked her. She reveals a world of hierarchies, humiliations, rules, and condescension; but these are increasingly mitigated by a new recognition that patients are human, that they pay the piper, and ought more often to be allowed to call the tune.

Much has been achieved in the last ten years by individuals and on the advice of the Ministry of Health. But only widespread knowledge and insistence on change can produce the revolution we are entitled to expect in the 1960s.

What's Wrong With Parliament?

Andrew Hill and Anthony Whichelow

Is Parliament receiving the right information to enable it to decide and control in the conditions of today?

The principal purpose of the House of Commons is – as it always was – to control public spending. Amid the complex legislation and astronomical budgets of a modern state, however, a busy debating-society of some 600 overworked members can be little more than a rubber-stamp, adding the initials of democracy at the foot of the government's bill. How, we may ask, can the unqualified representatives of the people presume to decide issues which may, at root, call for expert scientific understanding?

The two authors of this Penguin Special have made a close study of Parliament's workings. They believe this historic institution can be made to fulfil its intended function today, and they show how, with a fuller service of information, the Commons could be briefed to scrutinize more effectively the actions of the Executive. Their suggestions for improving that effectiveness are reasonable, practicable, and well-informed.

For a complete list of books available please write to Penguin Books whose address can be found on the back of the title page